# UNTANGLING YOUR RELATIONSHIP WITH MONEY

## A practical guide to move beyond money anxiety, fear and shame

# MARISKA REINERINK

Author can be reached at: mariska@yourmoneywellness.com

Untangling Your Relationship With Money/Mariska Reinerink. – 1st ed.

ISBN: 978-1-990830-50-1

# Contents

# Gratitude and Appreciation

While writing this book, I found myself reflecting on the profound journey that brought me to this moment. In every chapter, I am reminded of the incredible women, mentors, collaborators, and supporters who have shaped my path and made this endeavour possible. I wish to express my deepest appreciation to each and every one of you.

In your own way, you have helped me find my voice and blend my two worlds of physiotherapy and finance.

I extend special recognition, in somewhat chronological order, to those who have played pivotal roles:

**Deborah Price from The Money Coaching Institute.** Your certification program was precisely what my scientific brain needed to get the foundation to proceed. Learning from you, a visionary and pioneer in the field, has been a great honour.

Another pioneer in money coaching I have had the honour of learning from is **Kendall Summerhawk.** Becoming certified as a Sacred Money Archetype Coach and Money and Business Breakthrough Coach opened up a new world, providing me with impactful tools for working with my clients. Your passion, confidence, and determination have left an indelible mark on my approach.

I also want to thank other leaders in this field, **Bari Tessler, Denise Duffield-Thomas and Luna Jaffe.** Your books and podcasts have been instrumental in my growth. I am deeply grateful for the insights and perspectives you've shared.

A heartfelt thank you also extends to **Marie Salton and Sam Issari at the Vancouver School of Healing Arts** for inviting me to teach self-employment initially, which evolved into Professional Development - Business Mindset later on. This is where I got my first taste of teaching this material. Those classes helped me find my voice and get deeper insight into the mind-body-money connection.

Another instrumental part of my growth has been my collaboration with the **YWCA Metro Vancouver.** In particular, **Jennifer Bateman, Joann McKay, and Janice Lee** thank you for believing in me and offering space to empower women. Your request to create the Financial Literacy program for women was the catalyst for this book and created a clarity of purpose stronger than I had ever felt before. I love the brainstorming sessions with Jennifer and Joann on how to offer the program. It truly means the world to me, and I cannot thank you enough for believing in me.

Needless to say, this book would never have come into existence if it wasn't for the brilliant book coach and publisher **Suzanne Doyle-Ingram**! Your enthusiasm, patience, motivation and inspiration were the driving forces that brought this book into the world.

And, of course, I want to express my immense gratitude to my **clients and students** over all these years. Your confidence, loyalty and trust in me have been the foundation of my professional growth. Your journeys have shaped this book, and it is an honour to witness your successes. I look forward to many more meetings, workshops, classes and videos together!

Last, but definitely not least, a wholehearted thank you to my son **Dylan.** Your unwavering support, editing skills, brainstorming sessions, and constructive feedback have been priceless. I am immensely proud of the man you've become and grateful for your presence every step of the way. I love you!

Thank you all for being integral parts of my journey.

# Introduction

We've been taught that money is a numbers game and that if we just crunch the numbers and follow the rules, everything will fall into place. But if you've ever tried to budget or plan for your future, you know how much of a struggle it can be—and how much stress it can cause.

In my experience, having worked with people and money as a financial advisor for the past 20+ years, I have seen how the best-laid plans can fall apart because we ignore the human side of money. The stress and anxiety caused by dealing with money can overwhelm us. It can freeze us in our tracks. And when stress takes over our brain, logical thinking and common sense go out the window.

These are biological responses, and they all happen subconsciously, which is why they are often ignored. However, shedding light on our responses is not nearly as impossible as it may seem, and doing so can have a massive impact on our daily lives.

We all know that money makes us feel things: stress, worry, anxiety, guilt, relief, joy, empowerment... the list goes on. But when it comes time to pay bills or balance our chequebooks, those emotions get pushed aside in favour of just getting it done. Unfortunately, if we don't take time to understand where our feelings about money come from and why they're there in the first place, we'll never be able to process them and truly feel at ease with our finances.

That's because money is not just about numbers; it's also about emotions, beliefs, mindset, and so much more. It's about our perception of money, often more so than the reality of our finances. That perception determines how we feel, which in turn determines what we decide and how we act.

When we ignore our emotions and beliefs about money, they come up in ways that get us in trouble: panicked financial decisions, anxiety around spending and saving, being unable to have confident money conversations, and not feeling like the person we want to be with money.

So often, even strong, confident people—especially women—wobble when they get to the money side of life. Historically and culturally, money has been "men's business." Even in hunter-gatherer times, men were expected to be the providers and women were expected to focus on family and community, amongst other things. Given this, it's not surprising that navigating money, including the power that comes with it, can be particularly challenging for women.

In any case, our relationship with money can cause a lot of stress.

In my previous career as a physiotherapist, I saw the impact of money and money stress on people's bodies.

Often, people would be off work due to their health issue, which would have a financial impact. The money-related stress would increase the tension and slow down the healing.

It wasn't until later, after switching to a career in financial services, that I started to be able to connect the dots and figure out ways to offer help in a more holistic way.

Initially—in line with the idea that knowledge is power—I thought that helping people understand how money worked would help with money stress. Understanding money did help, to a certain extent. But there was still something I couldn't quite put my finger on until one day after volunteering at a single-moms group.

We had a particularly impactful session, where we didn't talk about specific financial topics but instead had a candid conversation about how money affected us. Lots of emotions came up. It was a wonderful, deep and open discussion. I remember walking to my car that evening and realizing that no amount of money in the world could "fix" all the anxiety, worry and shame that had come up—this all went way beyond money. That's when I had my lightbulb moment.

I had already worked in financial services for 15 years at the time, in the traditional way. I had already helped many people in all kinds of situations. But suddenly, I could see how our emotions and beliefs played a much more significant role in finance than we acknowledge.

I could see how we often confuse our self-worth with our net worth, and how guilt and shame derail even the best of us.

My own financial journey also showed me many examples of the impact of emotions. Even though I was very capable and comfortable helping other people with their finances and could come up with creative solutions for others, when it came to my own relationship with money, there was a lot of room for improvement.

Raising my son as a single mom, homeschooling him, and creatively fitting in my work in financial services wasn't easy. But on top of the stress of daily life, I realized I had certain beliefs that stopped me from being financially successful and comfortable. For example, I believed I could be successful or a good mom, but I couldn't be both. I thought making more than enough money meant working long hours and being away a lot. I wanted to be a good mom more than anything, and I couldn't see that jive with the long hours, so I didn't even try. (Luckily, I now know that this is not true, and have replaced it with the belief "work less, make more.")

So, I went on a mission to find out what that *other side* of money was and how it affects us. I had some amazing mentors along the way, and step by step, I healed my relationship with money. It was a life-changing adventure—I couldn't believe how deep some beliefs went! Through my own experiences, together with my research and studies, I've been able to bring together my experience as a physiotherapist working with the brain and nervous system and my 20+ years of experience in various roles in financial services, culminating what I share with you in this book.

I'm bringing this to you from an experiential side, as I've "been there, done that," and know how it feels. This book shares everything I've implemented to shift from barely surviving to thriving. I have since worked with thousands of women and some men to help them transform their relationship with money. I have seen what works, learned what doesn't, and continue to fine-tune the process. I am still amazed at the impact of this work, not just in someone's financial life but also in the rest of their lives, their confidence and how they show up in every other area of life. They walk taller, smile more and have a lightness that wasn't there before. That's what fills my heart!

My passion lies in empowering women to confidently handle the money in their personal and professional lives. I firmly believe that by supporting women in this way, I'm impacting not just individuals but entire families, communities, and, ultimately, the global community.

While I tend to work primarily with women, I want to emphasize that this information is equally beneficial for men. I've had the privilege of coaching several men and welcoming them into my workshops. If you are drawn to this book, I welcome you, regardless of gender. I hope the insights shared here will contribute to your personal growth and financial empowerment.

This adventure to illuminate the human side of money is a quest that goes beyond numbers and spreadsheets. It's a journey that asks you to look within and understand that money isn't just currency; it reflects your inner world. How money shows up in your life is a mirror that reveals your deepest beliefs and emotions.

My goal is to help you tap into more confidence and awareness when dealing with money, no matter what situation you're in today—whether you have very little money or more than enough.

Think of money as a person, and ask yourself, "How am I treating this person?". If it was a real person, would they stick around? What's the relationship I have with money? That's what we will explore in this book.

In the first four chapters, we'll dive into the biology and emotional roots of our relationship with money. We'll explore how our beliefs and emotions shape our financial reality.

The following chapters will show you how to apply this information in practical ways, unveiling how your beliefs and habits can manifest in your life. The human side of money is a dance between the rational and emotional, the tangible and intangible, and the practical and psychological aspects of our financial lives.

I have created this book to be an informative and practical guide, with plenty of worksheets to give you the opportunity to use your newfound awareness to discover your own beliefs and habits. You can download all the worksheets by going to www.yourmoneywellness.com/book.

I encourage you to start a money journal. This can be a dedicated notebook to write, draw and doodle what you need to express when exploring your relationship with money. If you choose, you can also use your money journal for the exercises in this book.

At the start of the book, you will find a section for your aha moments. It's essential to lock in and celebrate the new insights you gain while reading the book. Writing these down immediately will help deepen your understanding and solidify the new beliefs. If you want to use your money journal for this, please do. I suggest you create a separate section for aha moments so they are all in one place.

It's important to remember while reading that if I mention something that doesn't fit or resonate with you, don't try to make it fit. Sometimes, it's not yet time for that information to connect with you, and that's okay! It's a process, and there's a right time for everything. I am also hearing this from the women in my online course. Sometimes, they'll return to a previously watched video, and suddenly, it clicks. It just wasn't the right time when they first watched it.

The names of the people in my examples have been changed for privacy reasons.

I am truly honoured to be your guide on this journey. And to be clear, this book is for you no matter where you are on your money journey. Whether you have more than enough or not enough, this is the perfect time—this is YOUR time—so let's get started!

**All resources from the book**

www.yourmoneywellness.com/book

**The Money Wellness Blueprint course:**

http://tinyurl.com/378k4nk6

**Money Wellness Community on Facebook:**

https://www.facebook.com/groups/920065726207119

## AHA MOMENTS

It's so important to track the insights and aha moments you experience through life, as well as while reading this book. Make sure you keep this sheet handy so you can jot them down right away. Then use this to reflect on it later. You can also use it as a jumping off point for your journalling.

# Chapter 1

# Money Shame

When people start to talk about money, a common theme is the guilt and shame they feel around it. There are often discomfort and uneasy feelings that I'll group together under the umbrella term *money shame*. Since money shame can create a lot of chatter in our minds, making it harder to let in new information, we will start our journey by looking at money shame.

## What is Money Shame?

To begin, let's define what is meant by money shame.

At its core, shame is the profound sense of embarrassment or humiliation that leaves us feeling inadequate, like we're not good enough or should have done something better or different. It's a feeling that can arise when we think we've made a mistake or failed to meet our own or others' expectations.

When we introduce the concept of money to the equation, you get money shame. It is feeling like we've done something wrong with money or that we're handling money wrong, badly, or somehow not like we should.

When money shame comes up, we must ask ourselves questions to find out what it is based on: What standard are we holding ourselves to? Who decides how we should be with money? Who decides what's right and what's wrong?

It's not like we missed the class in school where all of this was discussed. Nope! There was no class in school where we really learned about money. We didn't get taught much (if at all) about money anywhere, not even the traditional topics like tax, saving and investing.

We may have learned about using a budget, but.... budgets don't work because they don't work with our brain and hormones. We'll explore how our brain processes money in Chapters 2 and 3.

You can find the video "Why Budgets Don't Work" on my website www.yourmoneywellness.com, under Resources.

When did we all begin to internalize this shame? Where did we pick up these often-unspoken expectations?

Most of our beliefs about money and our worth were picked up in childhood. We watched our parents handle this "thing" called money. We saw how they talked about it or avoided talking about it at all costs, how they fought about it and responded to it in stressful situations. Even though we may not have understood what money is or how it works at the time, we learned how to relate to it by observing all this.

The impact of our early experiences around money might even be stronger if our parents related to money quite differently from one another (as is often the case). One parent might have loved spending money, and the other might have wanted to save as much as possible, or be as frugal as possible. One parent might have loved making money and been highly resourceful, while the other wanted nothing to do with money. One parent may have been cool, calm and collected about money issues, even though the other was incredibly anxious about it. Let's not forget that our parents likely didn't learn much about money as they were growing up either!

We watched the adults around us, drew conclusions based on what we saw, and made subconscious decisions about money. These conclusions turn into beliefs over time, and we carry them with us into adulthood.

So far, in most societies and cultures, talking about money is still taboo. We don't discuss wages, our financial situation or how much we paid for something. And we usually don't discuss or even acknowledge our feelings and emotions around money, much less our sense of whether or not we deserve it.

In the meantime, we hold ourselves to an invisible, unachievable, undefined standard, and beat ourselves up for not achieving it! One reason we do this is that, often, somewhere along the line, we tied our self-worth to our net worth: I have money or don't have money; therefore, I am worthy / not worthy, successful / not successful. Then, we began to live life according to this belief. Is it any wonder money is such a loaded topic?

In a way, we're relying on money to solve the problem of not feeling worthy or successful. Money isn't the main issue, nor is it the solution.

Let's look at how money shame shows up.

As we're delving in, make sure you approach the inner work as an observer rather than feeling all the feelings. Being an observer will create a bit of distance between you and your thoughts and feelings and will allow you to see your patterns and underlying beliefs with more ease.

Self-talk fueled by money shame might sound like this:

- I'm bad with money.
- I'm bad at math.
- I have debt, so obviously, I'm terrible with money.
- I spend way too much money / I shop too much.
- I can't figure this out by myself.
- I'm not (strong/smart) enough.
- I'm embarrassed that I can't afford to do what my friends are doing.
- I'm afraid to look at my bank account balance.
- I'm too scared to ask for a raise or negotiate my salary.
- I'm ashamed that I'm in debt.
- I feel guilty for spending money.

- People won't like me if they know how much money I have.

- I'm overwhelmed by all this money stuff.

- I feel so guilty for being in this financial situation. I should have done a better job.

Do you recognize any of these?

What are your first thoughts when the topic of money comes up in conversation? You can write those down in your journal.

And remember, you're only observing! Don't beat yourself up for any of this. Most people feel some version of this and have similar self-talk. You are not alone!

## Physical responses

Usually, there's a physical response to money shame too. Here are some examples of what it can feel like:

- A **knot** in your stomach the moment you think about money

- **Sweaty palms**, even as you're picking up this book

- Getting **sleepy**, wanting to avoid the topic altogether

- **Heaviness or tightness** in your chest when you think about money

- **Feeling tense or irritable** when someone brings up the subject of money

- **Dizziness or light-headedness** when facing a financial situation

- Sense of **numbness or disconnect** dealing with your finances (avoidance)

- **Physical pain or discomfort**, like a headache or back pain, when you have to deal with a financial challenge or task

- **Wanting to cry** when the topic of money comes up

I'm not making these up. I've seen every single one of these, and many others, show up for people in my workshops, with my coaching clients and in the comments in my online course. And, of course, I've experienced them myself as well. It's pretty universal, no matter where you are in life.

Here are some more specific examples:

- Getting a knot in your stomach as you get closer to the checkout in the store because you're worried that your card might not be accepted, or because you think you are buying more than you need or "should."

- At a family dinner for the holidays, when the topic of money comes up, you want to get out of there, start feeling anxious, or tune out because money has been a topic that has always caused a lot of conflict and fighting in your family.

- Being unable to say no, such as when a friend asks you out for lunch, and you don't have the money for it, but go anyway because you're too embarrassed to say no. So you say yes, thinking, 'I'll figure it out later," even though you would have preferred not to go and spend the money.

- Getting taken advantage of financially because you are afraid to stand up for yourself.

Almost every single time, underneath the money shame, there's a belief that something is wrong with us. When I'm coaching my clients, this usually comes up as a version of...

"I'm not good enough."

Especially as women, it's something we tell ourselves a lot. It runs deep in many areas of our lives. And tying it back into money, "I'm not good enough" can be joined by the "I don't deserve" tape that often runs in the background.

## Shame keeps us small

Aside from the shame causing stress, which, as you'll learn, has a massive impact on our body and mind, it also keeps us small. It limits us and changes how we show up for people, as we're likely constantly running the tape of "I'm not good enough" or a version thereof in our head. Shame stops us from stepping into our power because we think we must stay small and invisible. As a result, we often withdraw from people and don't ask for help.

## How money shame can also show up:

One of my clients shared that she feels less than "rich people." She feels she's less deserving and not as "good" as them somehow. She also mentioned that when she's dating and considering a partner, she automatically deletes any wealthy guys because she feels that they wouldn't be a good match.

Another client shared that one of her colleagues had commented that my client appeared comfortable with her reduced, long-term disability salary. This frightened my client because it was accurate: She was more comfortable being "broke" than making solid money. After doing the exercise, she also realized she felt guilty for not having enough savings, and for having debt.

Often, money shame is also tied to not understanding the financial tools and systems as well. I hear people complaining about this all the time: "Money is so complicated."

But keep in mind that most information about finances was created by people who were almost certainly unaware of the human side of money. As a result, their approaches and advice were clinical and disconnected from reality. You can see why so many people struggle with their finances and don't have a financial plan... and feel shame around that.

Of course, money shame may show up differently for you. These examples are merely to show you money shame can sneak in in other ways as well.

----

Brené Brown explains shame well. She says shame needs three things to grow exponentially: secrecy, silence and judgment. If you think about it, that's the ideal recipe for money shame![1]

The taboo around money covers the **silence** part of that recipe.

And there's a lot of **secrecy** around money. For example, you're discouraged from talking about how much money you make.

There is also plenty of **judgment** about what people do with their money, whether it's someone's neighbour or the rich and famous. It's no wonder money matters often become breeding grounds for shame.

When it comes to judgment, we may worry about what we think others will say about our financial situation. But the judgment we have about ourselves is usually worse. It's not likely we would ever criticize a friend the way we criticize ourselves—we'd consider it too harsh. Yet judgmental thoughts keep looping in our minds.

---
[1] Brené Brown, Listening to Shame, Ted talk

## Your Turn

You might be thinking, "Great! Now that I've read all this, what do I do with the information?"

First, I hope you can see that it becomes easier to do something about it once you realize what's happening. You'll hear me talk about this many times in this book:

### AWARENESS IS POWER!

To get this awareness, let's see how money shame shows up in *your* life.

Yes, I'm assuming it's showing up for you, as usually there's some version of it. If there isn't, that's wonderful! I'd still recommend following along, just in case there's a sneaky way it has crept in.

I've created a worksheet to help you work through this and see what the impact of money shame has been for you.

### WORKSHEET

The first step is creating space for yourself to do this exercise. This is time for you!

Get comfortable... get a cup of tea or whatever you need. And remember, you're approaching this from an observer position.

You can write your answers in the book, in your money journal, or download the worksheet. It doesn't matter which method you choose, as long as you write it down. Don't just *think* it through! There's power in getting it on paper.

**If someone else could hear your self-talk, what you say to yourself about money, what would they hear?**

_____

_____

_____

_____

_____

**You can also tap into the physical symptoms: how does money shame show up for you? Where in your body do you feel it?**

_____

_____

_____

_____

_____

This is a fantastic first step to changing your relationship with money!

Next, give yourself some time to fill out the rest of the form.

How does money shame impact **you**?

_____

_____

_____

_____

How does money shame impact your **self-esteem**?

_____

_____

_____

_____

How does money shame impact your **confidence?**

_____

_____

_____

_____

Next, how does it impact your **kids and your family**?
Does it? If so, how?

_____

_____

_____

_____

How does money shame impact your **relationship**?

_____

_____

_____

_____

_____

Or your **work**? Do you show up differently at work because of money shame?

_____

_____

_____

_____

_____

And, of course, your **finances**: how does money shame impact your finances?

_____

_____

_____

_____

_____

**If you didn't have money shame, what would be different? Would you make different decisions? Would you spend differently? Save differently?**

_____

_____

_____

_____

_____

_____

_____

Now, sit back and **let this sink in**. What **insights** did you get from this exercise?

_____

_____

_____

_____

_____

_____

_____

Any **aha moments**? Make sure you jot those down on a separate sheet you can download at www.yourmoneywellness.com/book as well, or create a **separate sheet in your money journal**. This aha sheet will be an excellent reference for you as you continue reading the book. You'll see your progress and insights all in one place!

Is the impact of the money shame more or less than you thought?

_____

_____

_____

_____

_____

_____

_____

_____

_____

_____

_____

_____

_____

_____

## Next Steps

### ✓ Celebrate!

First of all, celebrate that you are now aware of money shame!

With this new awareness, you can catch yourself when it comes up. Take a deep breath, and then decide how you want to proceed. Questions you can ask yourself:

- Are there different ways to see this?
- Is this working for me?
- Am I holding myself back by thinking like this?
- What would feel better?

### ✓ Have compassion

Second, have compassion for yourself!

We are usually so much harder on ourselves than we are on others. So, let's turn that around: show yourself the same compassion and empathy you would show a friend in the same situation.

You might beat yourself up for not being great with money, but how could you have known any better? There really is nothing to be ashamed of. You are doing the absolute best you can do with the information you were given. There's no invisible standard we need to hold ourselves to!

Now that you have this new awareness about your self-talk and money shame, the next time you catch yourself thinking, "I'm so bad with money," or your version of it, stop and hug yourself!

I don't care if this might seem silly. **Just give yourself a hug as a genuine, physical reminder that you matter, you're doing the best you can, and that you are loved.**

Some of the participants in my course said they actually burst into tears with this step. It made them realize how hard they were being on themselves, and the hug was just the reminder they needed.

✓ **Start the conversation**

The third step is breaking the secrecy and silence and talking about the shame we might feel about money. When we talk about it, we stop the secrecy. That's when changes begin to happen. Talk about it! When you start to talk about money shame, you break the cycle of secrecy, not only for yourself but also for everyone else! It creates space for them to also break the silence.

When starting the conversation with family and friends, trust your gut feeling. *You* choose how open you want to be. Baby steps are fine. Be kind to yourself! Approach the conversation gently at first, because you are likely speaking to someone with their own baggage around money. Start talking about how *you feel* rather than the numbers.

For example, rather than saying yes to your friend's lunch request because you are scared of what she'll think when you say no, you CAN say:

"Actually, I've started working on my relationship with money, and right now, I really want to stick to my spending plan for the week. Can we do this next week?" ... or... "but I really would like to spend time with you. Can we have a picnic instead?" ... or ... "go for a walk instead?" Do NOT say, "because I don't have money" or "I can't afford it."

Even if that's true, it feels heavy when phrasing it that way, and it fuels the guilt and shame. There's no point in that. You are taking responsibility for your relationship with money now, and THAT is empowering!

I have heard SO many examples where friends react with relief, saying, "Thank God, I didn't want to spend the money either, but I didn't know what else to say."

If it feels like too big a step to start talking to your family or friends about this, join us in the Money Wellness Community on Facebook! You can find the link at www.yourmoneywellness.com/book. We're all there for the same reason: we want a better relationship with money. You could also start your own Money Wellness book club with like-minded friends where you can work through the exercises and discuss them in the group.

It will be so empowering to start having these conversations with people. Not only will it break the silence, but it will also confirm you're not the only one who's going through this. And it will bring all that is bubbling under the surface up to your awareness, where you can process it and begin to make new choices.

**Conversation starters/talking points for conversations about money:**

- What is the first emotion that comes up when you think about money?

- How was money in your life when growing up? *especially great question for couples

- Do you feel any money stress, and if so, how does it show up?

- Do you feel any money shame, and if so, how does it show up?

- Do you feel confident asking questions about money? Or, how do you feel when you ask questions about money?

Here are some more in-depth conversation starter ideas to help you connect with the important people in your life. These are my words and suggestions out of context, so feel free to adjust them to fit you:

- "Can I ask you something? I'm reading this book about money and our emotions (or money shame) and am realizing how many emotions and beliefs about myself I have tied to money. Do you find this too?"

  *The idea here is to create some context, which in this case is talking about what you've been reading/working on and then checking in with the other person about their experience. You may need more context or to say more about what you have discovered about yourself, but that will likely unfold as you talk.*

- "I usually feel pressured when it comes to... (buying birthday gifts for my friends / my kids' friends). What are your thoughts on this?"

  *This is based on what I've heard many people express regarding birthday gifts, holiday gifts, etc.: the dollar amount of what you "have to" spend seems to go up, and people go along to fit in. No one questions or stops the rising expectations. But once someone does, everyone is relieved, and a new agreement can be made.*

- "Can I ask you something? Instead of our regular get-together, would you be open to looking at another possibility? I've been reading about and working on my relationship with money and realize that I really enjoy spending time with you, but this expense that comes with... (lunch/ brunch/movies) is not something I want to put money towards at this time. Could we maybe go for a picnic instead / go for a walk instead / do you want to come to my place instead and I'll make us lunch / we'll have a visit there?

  *The idea here is to focus on what's important (spending time with your friend) but set some boundaries around the spending and offer options that do work for you—and likely for your friend, too—while still being able to spend time together. From here, a conversation about money, stress, etc., will probably flow, and you can start sharing.*

We can't cover every option here, but hopefully, you get a feel for how these conversations could go.

One caution: as you're starting out, pay attention with whom you choose to share. Everyone has their own money beliefs, comfort levels and willingness to talk and listen. Start with the easier conversations.

For example, if money has been a topic of heated discussions in your family for as long as you can remember, it might be helpful *not* to have your first conversation about money with a family member. There's likely too much history and too many triggers for everyone. Give yourself the time you need to work up to these money conversations. You may feel quite vulnerable, so why start with the hardest one? Go easy and work your way up from there.

Remember that compassion and empathy for yourself includes not putting yourself in situations that could be overwhelming.

**Action steps:**

### Celebrate your new awareness

How can you celebrate your new awareness? Go for a nice a walk? A nice cuppa tea and chocolate? A bath? Dance. To celebrate I will:

_____

_____

_____

### Compassion

I will have compassion for myself by:

_____

_____

_____

### Conversation

I want to start a conversation about money shame with:

_____

_____

_____

Join the Money Wellness Community on Facebook

## ONE STEP AT A TIME! YOU'VE GOT THIS!

## Summary

In this chapter, we covered the often-overlooked issue of money shame and talked about how addressing shame is the critical first step to improving your relationship with money. Money shame is the feeling of embarrassment or inadequacy related to how you handle money, and it usually stems from societal expectations and childhood experiences.

Money shame can manifest in self-talk and physical symptoms. And often, underneath it all is a belief along the lines of "I am not good enough."

Through the worksheet, you identified ways money shame is affecting you.

To deal with money shame, you can implement these action steps:

- **Celebrate your new awareness!** Awareness is key. With it, you can now ask yourself some questions to clarify where the shame in that moment is coming from.

- **Have compassion for yourself!** Give yourself a hug and remind yourself that you matter.

- **Start the conversation**. Breaking the silence around money will help you stand in your power while discussing money. It will also help you set boundaries and be your own money ally.

- **Join the Money Wellness Community** online to share your experiences, ask questions and celebrate your wins with like-minded people. You can find the link on www.yourmoneywellness.com/book

**You can do this! And in doing so,
you're helping everyone else, too.
Together, we can change the world,
one conversation at a time!**

# Chapter 2

# Money and Your Brain

In this chapter, we will find out the impact of money on our bodies. Or rather, the impact of our *perception* of money. And we'll start by looking at how our brains process money.

When it comes to money, there's an expectation we should be rational with money. That's the message we get all around us, whether at the bank, in the news, or talking with a financial advisor or that friend who seems to know "everything" about money. This expectation comes back to the general assumption that money is only about numbers. And if we're not "rational," we beat ourselves up for "not making good decisions" or "not being good with money"—which ties directly back into money shame! We beat ourselves up for not being as rational as we think we should be.

All of this completely ignores the fact that the 100 billion neurons, give or take, packed into your three-pound brain can generate an emotional tornado when you think about money. How we perceive money is closely linked to the evolution of our brain, and it's worth looking at.

I'm going to simplify the topic, leaving out all the nitty-gritty biological details, and paint a broad picture, highlighting the parts that matter to our relationship with money.

I hope that by understanding that our behaviour and feelings around money are closely connected to our biology—our brain and hormones—and that the biological processes all happen behind the scenes, you can start to understand why you might make the decisions you do. Then, you can let yourself off the hook and breathe a bit easier, especially if you're carrying a lot of guilt or shame around money.

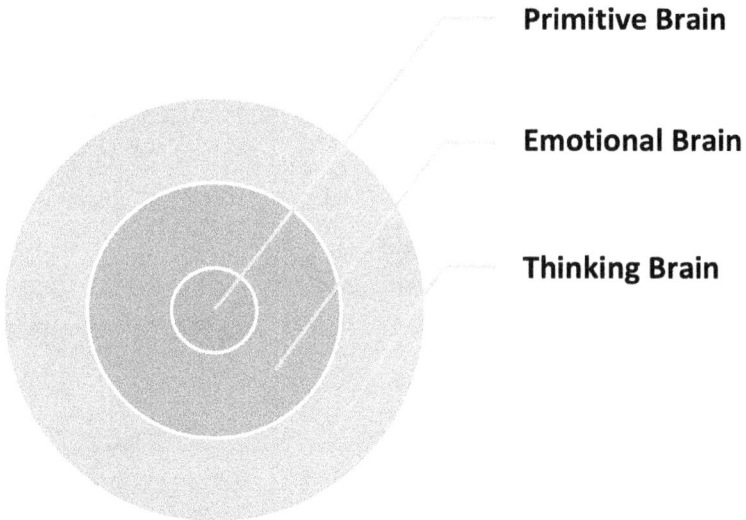

**Primitive Brain**

**Emotional Brain**

**Thinking Brain**

## Our Brain

### THE PRIMITIVE BRAIN

Millions of years ago, when humanity was just starting, our brain was a whole lot smaller and simpler. That brain is still part of our current brain. Let's call this the *primitive brain*. (It is also sometimes referred to as the *reptilian brain*.)

**The primitive brain is responsible for regulating essential functions**, like breathing, heart rate, hormone regulation, and basic instincts like the fight, flight, freeze or appease (FFFA) response.

All these bodily functions run in the background, controlled by our primitive brain on a subconscious or unconscious level. For example, you don't have to think about making your heart beat; thankfully, it does so automatically.

Survival mechanisms are also processed in the primitive brain. To effectively handle those FFFA responses, this part of the brain has to be lightning fast! This is a good thing because when you think of prehistoric times, or even now when faced with a dangerous, even life-threatening situation, it's crucial to respond immediately. You can't take your sweet time to analyze the situation. Your fight-or-flight instincts kick in, and your body just reacts.

And let's not forget about the often-overlooked components of the survival mechanism: freeze and appease. These are part of the same reflex. Think about it: how often do you find yourself frozen when in a panic? Or become extra friendly to avoid confrontation? We also do these things in situations that relate to money.

Other basic instincts also regulated by the primitive brain are fear and greed. They are primal responses. In the primitive brain, there's no room for language, numbers, common sense or logic. The primitive brain is all about lightning-fast reflexes and maintaining background processes.

## Interesting fact:

The primitive brain cannot distinguish between a real threat and an imagined threat. If we feel fear or stress about something that isn't really there, our brain and body still respond as if it were real.

Applying that to money, if you have certain fears around money—e.g., running out of money—your body will respond with a fear reflex, whether or not your fear is based in reality.

## THE EMOTIONAL BRAIN

As we evolved, our brain evolved as well and got a bit bigger. We now had more space to store information and, as a result, could store memories and emotions. We'll refer to this part as the *emotional brain*.

The emotional brain takes in the information from all our senses, filters it into *safe* and *not safe*, and works closely with the primitive brain to come up with a response. Emotions such as joy, anger and sadness provide valuable signals that guide our behaviour and help us navigate the world. However, when it comes to money, it can also put us at a disadvantage.

The emotional brain, together with the primitive brain, is where certain things get hardwired: memories and emotions from specific moments get stuck together in our brain. This can cause us to have intense reactions to something triggered by an unconscious memory or thought.

The more these thoughts and memories get repeated, the stronger the *neuropathway* becomes until it becomes automatic. (a neuropathway is a connection between the different areas of the brain).

Think of it like driving on a road with deep ruts or grooves. Once your tires get in a rut, it's hard to get out. But if you manage to get out of the rut yet continue to drive beside it, you only have to take your eyes off the road for a second to slip back in.

This is why many new beliefs you will create around money must be repeated many times, so you create a new groove! We'll cover this in an exercise later on.

> Both the primitive and emotional brains are lightning fast, work in the background and help keep us safe.

And then there's the *thinking brain*.

## THE THINKING BRAIN

As we evolved more, our brains expanded again to get us to where we are today. We now have even more "real estate" in our heads and can process much more complex information. We can use logic, common sense, conscious thought and reasoning to solve problems and make decisions. We have executive functions like planning, self-control and working memory.

The thinking brain allows us to consider long-term consequences and make complex decisions. It enables us to reflect, anticipate and have conscious control over our behaviour.

But because of all this processing power, the thinking brain is also quite a bit slower than the primitive brain, relatively speaking.

You might say, "This is all great, and the brain is truly amazing, but what does all of this have to do with money?"

Great question! Let's explore that!

Money, in its current form, has only been part of people's lives for the past few thousand years. What's important about this is that our brains haven't had much chance, biologically speaking, to adjust to or process the idea of money. More often than not, when the topic of money comes up, it triggers our primitive brain, as money is so closely linked with our sense of survival. And knowing what you know now about the different parts of the brain, do you think that's the part that should be in charge when it comes to money?

Probably not, right? Our thinking brain would be much better to make sense of things, see the bigger picture and apply logic. But remember how fast the primitive brain is? And the thinking brain not so much? When we think or talk about money, chances are the primitive brain gets triggered and makes a decision before the thinking brain has had time to process what's happening.

What I also find fascinating is that when we are in survival mode or feel stressed out, and the primitive brain is activated, blood flow to the brain decreases significantly. Some reports say the blood supply to the thinking brain may temporarily go down by 80%, as most of the blood goes to our limbs and the body parts vital to fight or flee.

Let's think about this: when you're in panic mode, which happens for many people when the topic of money comes up, your body responds in a way that takes your thinking brain offline since the blood is needed elsewhere. As a result, it is hard to apply logic, common sense, etc., *even if we want to!* We're simply not able to, from a biological point of view.

And yet here we are - criticizing ourselves, feeling shame or guilt about not managing money better, or whatever your version is. Do you see that, at the core, our approach to money is NOT a conscious decision and NOT something to blame yourself for?

Along with the guilt and shame, we typically experience anxiety and fear as well. Usually, the fear of not having enough. But remember that the primitive brain cannot distinguish between real and imagined threats or fears. It doesn't matter *to our brain* whether we really are in financial trouble or not -- it responds the same way.

I see this show up quite frequently when we don't have clarity about our money. We don't know how much is coming in or going out. Then fear kicks in, emotions take over, and as a result, the primitive and emotional brain are in charge. We *imagine/assume* we don't have enough without knowing if it's true or not. It *feels* true, so to us, it is. And, as I mentioned, our primitive brain responds the same to real and imagined threats.

Now, our body sends out stress responses like crazy, triggering the primitive brain and making it harder for our thinking brain to catch up. As a result, we can't think things through and access logic, common sense, or creative solutions. However, when we can slow down for a minute, work through the numbers and get clarity, the thinking brain can catch up, and the stress eases.

It's so much better to know the facts. Now you know for sure if you have enough money or not. Now, you can access the peace of mind that clarity provides. And you can stop reacting. It slows us down enough for our thinking brain to catch up. More about clarity in chapter 5.

## Your Turn

Let's see what part of your brain you use to make money decisions!

Sticking with the mantra "Awareness is power," think about the last few major financial decisions you made and write them down on the worksheet below or in your money journal.

Then write down which part of the brain made each decision. How did you feel at the time: calm and purposeful or stressed and anxious?

In hindsight, would you have made a different decision if you had felt more relaxed? We don't want to look back with regret, but seeing what we might have done differently, once we have some distance from our decision, can help us in the future.

|   | Money decision | Part of the brain |
|---|---|---|
| 1 | | |
| 2 | | |
| 3 | | |
| 4 | | |
| 5 | | |

You can also download the worksheet from
www.yourmoneywellness.com/book.

I've seen countless examples where, once we were able to take the stress level down a notch and talk, ask questions, breathe, and get to the numbers, it turned out that things weren't nearly as bad as they felt. And even if they weren't great, the person now had access to the logical, rational part of their brain, and finding solutions became more straightforward.

So, what we need is awareness to slow our primitive brain down just a little bit and give our thinking brain a chance to catch up.

## TIPS

Some tips to get your thinking brain online:

1. **Breathe:** the moment you notice you're in fight-or-flight mode, stop and take a breath. I know that can be easier said than done, but do what you can. Sometimes, this step alone is enough to break the cycle.

2. Once you're breathing consciously, **ask yourself these three questions**:

   a. What am I afraid of?

   b. Is this real?

   c. What are the facts?

These questions will allow your thinking brain to catch up and get out of fight-or-flight mode. Even if you don't have all the answers, it's okay!

Of course, being aware isn't suddenly going to change everything, but seeing the impact of engaging our thinking brain helps. What's done is done, and we can learn from that. Applying our newfound insight helps determine where some changes can be made.

There are more exercises to help with this after we talk about hormones.

## Summary

Thinking about money often triggers our survival mechanisms and, with that, our primitive brain and our emotional brain. When this happens, we can't access logic since rational thought is processed in the thinking brain. This helps explain why sometimes we do things that don't make sense in hindsight. As many of these brain functions are hardwired into our system, they run automatically until we pay attention to what's going on. Through awareness, we can more quickly recognize the feeling of fight-or-flight or panic, implement breathing exercises, or just hit the pause button for a minute. Doing any or all of these allows the thinking brain to catch up so we can make more informed decisions.

# Chapter 3

# Money and Your Hormones

Now that we know how the brain relates to our money decisions, it is essential to talk more about the connection with our body. The brain does not work in isolation; the body and brain function together. The stress response, for example, sets all kinds of other processes in motion.

In this chapter, we will look at the impact of our hormones and neurotransmitters (from now on, hormones for short) on money, and vice versa: the impact of money on our hormones.

Our bodies are home to many interactions and systems working together. And there are many different hormones, each with its own functions and roles to play. We will cover three key hormones here. Even learning a little bit about these three will make a difference:

- ➢ Cortisol

- ➢ Serotonin

- ➢ Dopamine

## Cortisol

Money stress ties money, our brain and our hormones together in many ways. When we experience stress, our body releases cortisol to prepare us for what's happening. As a result, our heart rate increases, our blood pressure goes up, we begin to sweat and breathe faster and our muscle tension increases.

It's a normal, helpful process, and if it's a one-time situation, there's no problem. It's actually crucial for us all this happens when necessary.

For example, if you almost got into an accident, your cortisol levels would go up, and you would experience many of the symptoms I just mentioned. It's a normal response, and with time, your cortisol levels would naturally return to base level.

But if you had chronic stress and, as a result, chronically high cortisol levels, it would become problematic.

For many people, the topic of money causes a stress reaction. And because money is part of almost every aspect of our lives, we bump into this stress-producing topic many times a day, triggering a stress response and cortisol production each time.

Maybe it's just a little blip, but still, it's a stress response. The cortisol level often doesn't get a chance to go down again before the next trigger shows up. We get dose after dose of cortisol in our body, and it accumulates.

When the body is constantly overloaded with cortisol, we do experience the previously mentioned symptoms (increased heart rate, blood pressure and muscle tension; faster breathing), but chronic cortisol overload creates additional symptoms as well.

Common symptoms of cortisol overload:

- ☐ Difficulty relaxing
- ☐ Don't stay in one place long or restless
- ☐ Over-caretaking
- ☐ No off button / workaholic
- ☐ Fatigue
- ☐ Memory fog
- ☐ Weight gain around the abdomen
- ☐ Hypervigilance

Do you recognize any of these in yourself? Have a look at the symptoms to see which ones you recognize, especially regarding you and money.

Please note: we're not doing this exercise to diagnose anyone or anything but rather to start recognizing these stress responses and their impact on our lives.

I want to elaborate more on hypervigilance, as it's such a common feeling, yet not necessarily a common term. Hypervigilance is when the brain constantly scans the surroundings, looking for potential danger or threats. I often hear women in my workshops talk about "waiting for the other shoe to drop." Or they describe a feeling of holding their breath, ready for the "next disaster."

Hypervigilance is a stress reaction that creates a vicious cycle. When a person constantly imagines things going wrong and expects the worst, the primitive brain interprets this as a threat. As a result, the body produces even more cortisol.

We'll learn how to break that cycle later on in this chapter.

When cortisol levels are high, it affects the overall hormone balance quite a bit. High cortisol can cause serotonin levels to drop.

## Serotonin

Serotonin is our feel-good hormone. It gives us the sense that all is well in the world. It helps us sleep well, helps with our memory, and promotes a sense of calm and relaxation, amongst other things. Serotonin is critical in promoting emotional well-being and regulating mood, sleep, appetite and other bodily processes that contribute to our overall functioning and quality of life. It's an essential hormone for good health!

However, chronically high cortisol levels impact serotonin function and availability and often cause serotonin levels to go down. With lower serotonin levels, we don't feel so great, to put it mildly. Our moods change; we don't sleep as well; we might feel anxious and even start to feel depressed.

But our bodies are amazing at finding ways to cope, and to make a complex story short, we may, subconsciously, go to the hormone dopamine for some relief.

## Dopamine

Dopamine is the reward and pleasure hormone. It gives us a sense of euphoria and excitement. It feels like a natural high. We feel wonderful and on top of the world! It also helps with motivation and learning and gives us the determination to accomplish goals, look for rewards and take action.

Dopamine plays a vital role in our well-being, but if there's an imbalance, it can create problems.

Returning to reduced serotonin, where we don't feel so great, we may look for ways to get our system to produce dopamine—subconsciously, of course. What can we do to feel better?

Well, one of the things that gives us a dose of dopamine is shopping! Ever heard of retail therapy? Even if you don't go impulse shopping for fun and likely unnecessary items, dopamine plays a role even when you do something as common as shopping for groceries. (There are other unbalanced ways to stimulate our bodies to produce dopamine, like gambling, eating, drugs and alcohol, but we'll stick to shopping for now.)

Several studies have shown that when we go shopping, especially when we find a good deal, the different brain areas connected with pleasure, reward and dopamine release are strongly activated.

We get a natural high and feel great (you know the feeling, right?)—we're on top of the world! For a short time, at least. However, the issue with dopamine is that the effects don't last long. Once you have bought whatever you wanted to buy, the dopamine effects wear off; you're back to low serotonin levels and high cortisol levels.

The hormone imbalance might be even worse now since you've just been shopping and have bought something on impulse. It's like a double-whammy once the credit card bill comes in: still too much cortisol, not enough serotonin and no more dopamine, so we feel crappy again. And we now have a credit card bill to pay or less money in our account. To cheer ourselves up, we might just go shopping again.

This behaviour doesn't come from the logical part of the mind, the thinking brain. It's much more subconscious and connected to the primitive brain, where logic and common sense don't exist. It can quickly turn into a vicious cycle where you keep going back to shopping to feel better, but never really do in the end, as shopping doesn't address the underlying problem: money stress and an unhealthy relationship with money. You must "get" dopamine to feel better or even half-decent. It's not great for your body or your finances.

Do you recognize any of this at all? What I've described might be a fairly intense scenario, but you might recognize some version of it.

**The problem with dopamine-fuelled shopping is that you buy something because you want to *feel better*, not because you need the item!**

We are trying to solve a problem with a solution that doesn't fit.

The solution for this is to manage our money stress by addressing our relationship with money, and finding healthier ways to feel better.

On the other hand, you *can* use this to your advantage: if you do need to buy something, buy it on sale. You'll get the item you need *and* will have spent less money, *plus* you'll get some extra dopamine out of it all.

Luckily, there are also some healthy ways to get dopamine:[2]

- Meditating
- Creating a daily to-do list
- Having long-term goals
- Eating foods high in L-tyrosine, high-protein food such as chicken, turkey, fish, milk, yogurt, peanuts, almonds, pumpkin seeds, sesame seeds, soy protein and lima beans.[3]
- Exercising regularly
- Creating something, like writing, music or art

## Your Turn

Now that you can see how some of your money decisions may be dopamine fuelled and not helping your financial situation, what can you do instead?

---

[2] www.mindmypeelings.com

[3] https://en.wikipedia.org/wiki/Tyrosine

The solutions all have to do with reducing money stress. You're already taking a significant step by reading this book and working on your relationship with money. Beyond that, here are some things you can implement right away based on what we covered in this chapter:

## 1. Make a Happy List

The Happy List is a list of things that make you feel better, at ease, and calmer. These are things that help you breathe and get out of survival mode. Even if it's just for a few minutes - that's often enough to break the cycle and get your thinking brain caught up.

## STEPS:

1. Download and print out the list (www.yourmoneywellness.com/book) or use the one at the end of the chapter

2. Write down your own list of various things that help you relax and feel good, so you can choose what fits best when you need a boost. Ideally, put things on the list that don't cost money, or at least not a lot. We want to break the connection between spending money and feeling better!

3. Put the list up in a good spot with easy access.

4. Next time you need a boost or want to go shopping to feel better, stop, go to your list, pick something that you want to and can do at that moment, and then do it!

Some of my favourites are going for a walk (by the beach if possible), dancing to my playlist with all my favourite dance songs, curling up on the couch for 30 minutes with some lovely tea and a good book, doing yoga, watching a good movie, having a bath, drawing/painting, meditating/listening to a sound bath and having a nap. (Don't underestimate the power of naps!)

Find out what works for you. If you don't know, because you've never had the chance to think about what *you* want, just try different things and see what works for you.

## 2. Self-care routine

Because we've talked a lot about the impacts of stress, it makes sense that looking after ourselves is vital to having a better relationship with money, even though it might seem counterintuitive.

Often, when we experience money stress, or a feeling of scarcity or not-enoughness, our instant reaction is to do more, run faster and work harder. I hope you can see from what we've discussed in this chapter that this is a cortisol reaction. It's a stress reaction, and it shuts down your thinking brain. It shuts out your logic and also your creativity. So, calming down your nervous system to reduce your stress is crucial.

We need to break that cycle and let our stress levels come down, even just a little bit. That way, we take care of ourselves first and don't run on empty. Think of the instructions you get when flying: put on your own oxygen mask before you help anyone else.

Implementing a self-care routine is one way to break that cycle. Self-care will allow your stress levels to decrease. Then, your thinking brain will be able to catch up, and you can access your creativity better and come up with some fantastic solutions! Most of all, you will feel better. And everything else just gets a little bit easier when you feel better. Right?

**Self-Care Routine**

Commit yourself to start with 15 minutes a day.

This is YOUR time!

You deserve it!

No matter what, commit to self-care. Aim for at least 15 minutes in the beginning, and increase the time if you can. If even that seems impossible, then start with 5 minutes. Just start the habit! Start with what you can and build from there.

**This step ties into the Happy List since you can choose activities for your self-care time from that list**. Your activities don't have to be the same every day, but if you like the routine of it, then stick to one or two activities. The key is to do what works for you!

**Put your Happy List and Self-care list on your bathroom mirror or bedroom door so you are reminded of it frequently.** I suggest that you do your self-care activity even before you reach for your cell phone in the morning or start planning your day.

### 3. Journal it

Write about what you've realized from reading about money, your brain and your hormones, as well as the realizations you have about your stress levels and their impact on your money.

By writing it all down, you're processing it and will be able to reflect on it later. Otherwise, it just swirls around in your head and messes up your thinking. Get it out on paper, and then you can look at it with a bit of distance.

This is a vital part of creating awareness!

## Summary

When we experience stress, including money stress, our body produces cortisol (amongst many other hormones/neurotransmitters).

Chronic levels of high cortisol reduce our serotonin, our feel-good hormone. When this happens, we don't feel so great, and we may seek out dopamine-producing activities to get that natural high from dopamine (even temporarily), which can turn into a vicious cycle of spending more money to feel better.

As mentioned, this is a simplified version of what happens. Of course, many other systems are involved, as are many other hormones and neurotransmitters.

To manage this stress cycle, you can:
1. Make a Happy List and use it whenever you need a boost.
2. Self-care: start with 15 minutes a day.
3. Journal and clear your mind.

What makes you happy in an instant? If you don't know, try out some things from the self-care list.

# YOUR HAPPY LIST

✓ _____

✓ _____

✓ _____

✓ _____

✓ _____

✓ _____

✓ _____

✓ _____

✓ _____

✓ _____

✓ _____

✓ _____

✓ _____

✓ _____

✓ _____

✓ _____

✓ _____

✓ _____

Here's a list of self-care ideas to get you started. Feel free to add your favourites too!

| Category | Self-Care Ideas |
| --- | --- |
| **Physical Health** | |
| | Take a 10-minute walk |
| | Practice deep breathing exercises |
| | Stretch for 5 minutes |
| | Enjoy a healthy snack |
| | Take a power nap |
| | Sleep in for an extra hour |
| | Sit outside for 30 minutes |
| | Dance to your favourite songs |
| | |
| **Mental Well-being** | |
| | Practice mindfulness meditation |
| | Write in a journal |
| | Listen to calming music |
| | Declutter a small space |
| | Learn a new relaxation technique |
| | Practice positive self-talk |
| | Take time for solitude |
| | No social media for the day |

## Emotional Wellness

Engage in a favourite hobby

Connect with a friend or family member

Watch a funny movie or show

Express appreciation in a journal

Allow yourself to cry if needed

Write down 3 things you like about yourself

Ask for what you really need

## Relaxation techniques

Take a warm bath or shower

Use aromatherapy or essential oils

Listen to a guided meditation

Practice box breathing (4-4-4-4)

Go for a slow, mindful walk

Do 2 rounds of EFT tapping (find on youtube)

Stretch for 10 minutes

Listen to a sound bath (e.g. spotify)

# Chapter 4

# Money and Your Past

As you've probably already figured out, there's a lot more to money than meets the eye. Most of it happens below the surface, in our subconscious. To further explore what we carry in our subconscious about money, we will look at our past.

How we relate to money in the present has everything to do with what happened in our past.

Research shows that many of our beliefs about money are formed during childhood, particularly before the age of 15.

For example, a study by the University of Michigan found that children as young as five already had distinct emotional reactions to spending and saving money, which later translated into actual spending behaviours.[4]

This also illustrates the hardwiring I mentioned in Chapter 2 about money and the brain: if something happens to us when we're little—let's say a bee sting—

_____
[4] https://www.cnbc.com/2021/12/17/four-unhealthy-beliefs-about-money-you-may-have-learned-from-childhood.html

the pain and the emotions we felt at that time get stored in our brain and connected with the image of the bee. The next time we see a bee, our bodies react immediately by creating a stress response based on past fear and pain. Our early memories of money, especially seeing how our parents or caregivers dealt with it, can shape our beliefs and behaviours in a similar way.

For example, my client Katie remembers always saving her allowance diligently, whereas her sibling would spend it immediately at the candy store. Katie would tuck her money away in a container next to her bed and feel great about it. She'd dream about a toy she was saving for and looked forward to having enough money to buy it. However, at one point, her parents needed money and took her little stash away without asking or telling her. This left her feeling sad, powerless and defeated. She had been so diligent to save the money, and now it was gone! Another time, her brother stole some of her money to spend it on something. She was furious at her little brother and again felt sad and powerless.

As we worked through this memory, she discovered that, in those moments, she subconsciously concluded that "money can be taken away at any point, and I have no power or control over it."

That evolved into a belief that "there's no point in saving because it will just be taken away anyway... so why bother?" But this clashed with her original joy of saving money, which is what she really wanted and enjoyed.

As a result, there was a tug-of-war between "why bother" and "I love to save," and her money habits would swing from impulse spending to tremendous anxiety about not having enough money saved.

This is precisely where Katie was when we met: no savings and feeling insecure and anxious, feeling that any money she did have could be taken away at any point. With the help of the coaching process, she was able to disconnect the emotional trigger from the memory, her anxiety levels went down considerably, and her relationship with money improved.

Another example comes from my client, Lauren, who remembers her parents not talking about money at all. There was a lot of stress in her parents' relationship. When her mom got stressed, or after a fight with the dad, she would grab the kids and take them shopping. As a child, Lauren thought this was wonderful. But subconsciously, the connection was made: shopping was a way to deal with stress. Unsurprisingly, in her adult life, Lauren also uses shopping as stress relief. After what we covered in Chapter 3 about hormones, you'll recognize the impact of dopamine here.

Another example of the past influencing the present is my client Josie, who recalls family dinners turning into huge debates and heated discussions/fights about money. As one of the younger siblings, she would shut down and try not to be part of these arguments. In her adult life, Josie sees money as a source of contention and chaos. She wants to avoid it at all costs. She experiences a lot of stress just thinking about money or looking at her statements, and she prefers bartering over an exchange of money. So, we've had to work through the process of disconnecting the emotion from the memory—and then creating a new belief around receiving money, one that feels positive and good.

The memories don't always have to have a direct connection to money. Sometimes, it's about being seen, or rather not being seen, or feeling like you don't matter, which in our adult life can show up as a form of "I'm not worthy."

I see this as well in people with traumatic childhoods. For example, those who grew up in a household with violence or alcoholism.

I often hear from those clients that, as kids, they always had to scan their environment and the people in it to see what was going on and constantly anticipate what would happen. Can you sense the intense fight, flight, freeze or appease readiness here?

They would then quickly decide if they could stay, needed to do something, or needed to run and hide. There wasn't space to think about what they wanted. It was about keeping themselves safe by giving the other the other person what they needed.

My client Emily shared her experience of seeing her (alcoholic) dad's car pull up. Even before he entered the house, she would already know how bad the situation was and determine if she could cheer him up and change his mood, or if it was beyond that point, requiring her to hide in her room to ensure the safety of herself and her siblings.

Experiences like this affect the way people both spend and receive money throughout their lives. These children never got to ask themselves what they wanted, needed, or how they felt. They were left with subconscious beliefs like "I'm not safe," "I'm not worthy," or "I don't deserve." These patterns often show up in adulthood as overspending, indecisiveness, over-giving, impulsiveness or restlessness.

Such patterns result, in large part, from constantly checking what the other person needed versus what they needed. They correlate to the primitive brain and the stress response we discussed in previous chapters. People who grew up with high cortisol levels will likely have a dopamine imbalance behind their stress-induced behaviours.

## Staying small to stay safe

Another influence from the past I see often is the trauma response: staying small to stay safe. If something terrible happened to us as a child, it may create a belief that we'll get hurt if we are seen, causing us to stay small to stay safe. A simple way of explaining this is that staying small makes us less visible, which we connect to being safe, as the person or situation that might hurt us can't find us. This way, we avoid getting hurt and experiencing pain or an unsafe or uncomfortable situation.

When I first learned about this response and realized the impact it was having on my life, I was surprised to see it tied into money as well. Somehow, my brain had translated it into "if I don't have money (= stay small), then I'm safe."

Of course, it's not a logical conclusion. Even though it might have been an effective coping mechanism when we were younger, in our adult lives, coping mechanisms like these are not helpful anymore. That's why it is so important to be aware and to re-evaluate which beliefs still serve us and which do not.

Sometimes, the impact of money in our past doesn't come from our parents or behaviours we witnessed, but rather from the impact of not having enough money or "too much" money. Yes, I've seen this happen too!

For children who grew up in (extreme) poverty, the memories and hardwiring can be around being teased at school because of what they were wearing. Or where they lived compared to the other families. Or not wanting to invite friends over because of their home situation. In these cases, there tends to be a lot of shame carried into adulthood. The beliefs that are held along with the shame might be "I'm not good enough" or "I don't matter."

For those who grew up feeling that they, or their family, had too much money, the weight that can come with the feeling of having money is no less impactful than not having money. For example, as children, they might have been aware that their family had more money than their friends' parents and would try to hide it to fit in. Or their parent(s) might have cared a lot about status and showing off their wealth, which could result in the kids feeling embarrassed by that and going in the opposite direction during adulthood. Or they would see it as the way to behave and take that on themselves. Or the parents would model that money is more important than people, resulting in the kids feeling they didn't matter, or feeling that money was the only way to be accepted and seen.

One of my mentors coached a man who grew up in an affluent family. He had always heard his dad say that if you don't make more than $50 million a year, you're a loser, or something along those lines. When he started the money coaching journey, his brother made more than $50 million a year, but he only made $46 million a year and didn't have a private plane like his friends did. He felt like a "total loser." He experienced money stress and shame as well and had to work through his old beliefs, too.

This goes to show that the common perception that if you have money, you don't have money stress or shame isn't true. The stress of having money can look different than for someone who is struggling to make ends meet, but it's stress, nonetheless. It still impacts our bodies and self-esteem, self-talk and everything else in the same way!

## Allowances

Another way some beliefs around money can creep in is when it comes to allowances.

Often, kids get allowances. In theory, there's nothing wrong with that. However, allowances often get tied to a performance or behaviour: you must do your chores to *earn* the money. Or you have to be on your best behaviour to *deserve* the allowance. Alternatively, you don't get your allowance because you didn't do your chores or misbehaved.

This can lead to a belief that if we are "good," we get money. And if we are "bad," we don't. In our illogical, primitive brain, this can transform into "I don't have money, so I must be bad" or "I am bad with money." Or "I have to be extra good if I want more money," which can turn into "If I want more money, I must work harder, try harder, be more helpful."

This can set kids up for unhelpful money beliefs and behaviours down the line, even though the parents never intended any of that to happen.

## What can you do instead?

Giving kids an allowance is excellent, as it teaches them about money from an early age. They can learn about the value of money and what it can do for them. They can know it's a tool and doesn't define them as a person.

Having kids take on specific tasks in the house is also fantastic. They learn the value of time and looking after their surroundings. And about contributing to their own well-being and that of the family.

Connecting the allowance and the chores, however, is where it might get messy.

They might learn not to do anything unless they get paid for it. Or learn that you have to be "good" to get paid and vice versa. Or it might turn money into a power struggle: the parent has the money, and the child has to do what they're told if they want to get any of it.

A better option would be to keep the two separate, with clear communication about both.

As you're working on your relationship with money and start to see your own triggers, beliefs and patterns, clear communication about money with your kids will also become easier. You'll be able to see money as something that's separate from you and doesn't define who you are.

## Your Turn

Now that you've read some examples of how our past can and does impact our present money beliefs, let's explore your money history. Doing a mini money bio is an excellent way to get insights into your memories.

Maybe your money history isn't as dramatic as in the examples I used. That's totally fine. This is not a competition. It's about the impact money had on you back then. It's about creating awareness of your beliefs. Remember: awareness is power!

### Mini Money History

First, find some time and a quiet spot so you're not interrupted. Use either the space in this book or download the worksheet. (www.yourmoneywellness. com/book)

Grab your favourite pen. Take some deep breaths. Feel your body. Feel grounded. Feel present.

Then think back to your childhood, as far back as you can remember. Think of the five strongest memories from your childhood that come up for you around money. Money may be directly or indirectly involved. Go with what comes up. Don't judge it. Don't filter it yet.

Write your memories on the worksheet in the left column. If many memories surface (way more than five), briefly write down all the memories you remember. When you're done, look at them and circle the earliest ones. From there, pick out the five that resonate most with you—the ones with the strongest emotions—as they lay the foundation for the later memories.

Sort them chronologically and then write about each of those five memories in as much detail as possible:

➤ What happened?

➤ How did that situation make you feel?

➤ What did you think at that moment, and after?

➤ Did this situation happen often, or was it a one-time occurrence?

➤ If it happened frequently, did you interpret it differently as time passed?

➤ Do you have some idea about what conclusion you drew from that situation?

Write as much as you can. Also, mark your age (approximate) at the time of that event. Ideally, you'll have the memories on the worksheet in chronological order. In this way, you can sometimes start to see the connection between the memories. Then, move on to the next memory and follow the same steps.

If you're having a hard time accessing those memories, here are some tips:

- If you grew up speaking a different language, you may want to switch to thinking in that language to access the memories better.

- Think of it by decade. For example, what do you remember from before you were 10, from when you were between 10 and 20, and so on?

- Or think about events:

  o Who was in charge of money in your family? How did that affect you?

  o How were birthdays celebrated? Was there a party? Gifts? How did you feel receiving those gifts?

  o Did you get an allowance, and how did that work if you did?

  o Did you fit in financially at school?

  o Did you go on holiday with your family? If so, what were those holidays like? If not, how did your family spend time together?

o Did your parents talk about money between themselves? And to you? Did they teach you about money?

o Did you have a job in your teens, like babysitting, a paper route, washing cars or something else? If so, what did you do with the money?

Once you're done with the money bio, look at all the memories that bubbled up:

➢ Is there a mix of happy ones and not-so-happy ones?

➢ Do you see similarities?

➢ Do you see a pattern? Or a progression?

➢ And the most important question is, do you recognize any of these emotions or patterns in your life right now? Do you still carry them with you?

Remember: NO judgment! You've done the best you could with the tools you had. We're only doing some reconnaissance here. Have compassion for yourself!

This exercise is all about creating awareness so that we can break the invisible hold that money memory has over us.

Now go to the Aha Worksheet and write down any aha moments you had from doing this exercise and any insights or realizations you got from it. Writing these down is crucial so you can reflect on them later and help your brain process it all. This work doesn't have the same impact if you do it as a mental exercise without writing anything down. We need to see our thoughts and feelings on paper to get some distance from them. And more clarity!

To finish this exercise, take a moment to acknowledge yourself for having the courage to delve into your money bio. Since avoiding money is so ingrained in our culture, it isn't for the faint of heart to take this on. Kudos to you! You've got this and taken another big step on your money journey!

## BONUS

If you want to delve deeper into your money past, you can take one of the memories that feels like it had the most impact. Then, play it in your mind like a movie and take on the director role. Start with the time leading up to the scene you remember in your money memory. Review what happened. When you get to the scene that felt uncomfortable, ask yourself what you could change in that scene to make it feel better.

For example, do you need to insert the adult you as another player in that scene to put the younger you at ease? Do you need to insert a different dialogue? You can even add yelling at the person if that helps. Or have your parent stand up for you and keep you safe. Maybe bring in an object to help with the situation.

One of my clients inserted a hot air balloon she could step into and float away from the situation. Another inserted herself as the adult and helped steer the situation into a much better outcome. Whatever works, right?! It's in your imagination, so you're not limited by reality and practicality.

Whatever the solution, the effect you're looking for is how you *feel* when you imagine the new scene. If you feel better, then you're onto something. Keep playing with the pieces until it feels right. Use anything you need to break the direct link between the fear, panic or powerlessness you felt, and money. For example humour: If you end up making the whole situation silly and crack up every time you think about it, you've achieved the goal of rewiring the connection between the old memory, the old emotion and your belief.

From there, it's like a pebble thrown in a pond: the ripple effect will work through your system, and you'll start seeing subtle changes in your relationship with money.

If, for some reason, you're getting stuck or frustrated along the way, don't worry. Stop, go for a walk and come back when you're able. Listening to your body and working through what might surface is essential.

**Worksheet:**

What are the five strongest memories from your childhood?

| Your money memory | Emotion(s) | Conclusions |
|---|---|---|
|  |  |  |
|  |  |  |
|  |  |  |
|  |  |  |
|  |  |  |

Describe the scene you remember in the left column. Then focus in on the emotions that came up for you in that memory. Write those in the Middle column. Then think about what conclusions you may have drawn in those moments.

These conclusions you made in the past have been with you, in your subconscious, since then. Looking at your relationship with money now, and how money shows up in your life currently, can you see any connections?

**Write your reflections and insights below**

_____

_____

_____

_____

_____

_____

_____

_____

_____

## Summary

In this chapter, we explored the impact of our childhood experiences on our current beliefs and relationship with money.

Most of our money beliefs are formed during childhood, before the age of 15. And we carry them with us in our subconscious into adulthood.

There were various examples to show you a range of possible scenarios and help you better understand how the past and present are connected, in relation to money.

In the Mini Money Bio exercise, you dove into your own past and filtered out the five strongest memories regarding money and your past. With this new awareness, you are already gaining new insights into your current relationship with money.

The bonus exercise suggested you recreate an impactful scene from your past in a way that feels better, safer and more empowered. Doing this exercise will rewire your brain, which will then update your beliefs and relationship with money.

# Chapter 5

# Money Clarity

So far, we have looked at the human side of money and what goes on in our bodies and minds regarding money.

We discovered how money shame can keep us small, and that emotions like fear and anxiety can throw us off track when managing our finances. Additionally, we learned that money stress can mess with our spending by affecting our hormones. And that the beliefs we develop during childhood may run constant interference in the background, causing us to repeat the same unhelpful patterns and behaviours with money.

All of this affects how we handle money: how we bring money in, how we spend it and how we save it.

The exercises you did in the previous chapters helped you become more aware of your patterns and behaviours. I hope you have gained valuable insights into your relationship with money already and feel more confident, excited and hopeful as a result.

But what about the practical side of money? How do we connect the dots between our emotions and the dollars and cents?

Not only do things like money shame and old beliefs impact how we feel, but they are connected with the practical side of our money too. By looking at our numbers, we can get an even better picture of our patterns and behaviours.

So often, though, we avoid looking at our financial situation. Sometimes, this is because we fear what we'll discover. Or it could be because we don't know where to start and feel overwhelmed by it all.

The result is that we have no idea where we stand financially. Maybe we have enough, maybe we don't. But we feel crappy about money, scared or intimidated, so we avoid it. It's a totally normal reaction! Why would we want to do something uncomfortable or intimidating? Something we tell ourselves we're bad at?

Combining money shame, our emotions and self-talk stemming from our beliefs about money, we arrive at a perfect setup for avoidance — which only makes matters worse because the impact of not knowing your numbers is considerable.

You see, without clarity on the numbers, it's like trying to navigate in the dark. We don't know if we're financially A-okay or teetering on the edge. "Should I make that big purchase or hold off? Do I need to cut back, or can I afford it?" Without a grip on the numbers, it's a guessing game. And that leaves way too much room for our emotions to take over: fear can set in, and we can freeze up.

The result of not having clarity, and the uncertainty that comes with it, is that we often feel we can't move forward. We feel stuck. It's like getting stuck in *financial quicksand*. We feel like we have no solid footing. Without solid footing, every decision feels like a risky step. And if we try to move, it sucks us in deeper.

Let's apply this to money decisions: if you lack clarity about your financial situation and make a decision anyway, it can intensify your uncertainty and trigger more fear and anxiety, causing you to freeze even more. It can become a vicious cycle: you *know* you need to decide or take action, but the fear and anxiety can be overwhelming.

Interestingly, I've witnessed this at all income levels, not just lower income levels, as you would expect. The brain works the same way regardless of income. If we don't have clarity about our numbers, it doesn't matter how much we make. Our brain is always going to lean towards the negative, fearing the worst.

Our brain is wired this way! We're wired to notice and dwell on negative events more than positive ones. The negatives tend to carry more weight and impact us more than the positive ones. Don't worry, it's not just you, it's all of us—a quirk of human psychology.

Escaping the clutches of financial quicksand hinges on getting a crystal-clear picture of your financial situation so you can see exactly where you are, regardless of what the situation may be.

Some examples to give you some insight into the impact of not having clarity are:

A couple asked me to do a retirement plan for them. They told me how afraid they were of the results and that it wouldn't surprise them if they'd have to eat canned cat food for dinner in retirement. They were joking, sort of, but you could tell that they were really worried about not having enough money to retire. The stress and worry were palpable!

To see if this worry was real or imagined, we gathered the numbers, and I entered them into my retirement planning software. Much to their surprise, they were closer to having enough money to retire than they thought they were. And by being able to put away another few hundred dollars a month, they would be on track for the retirement they wanted.

Their relief was immediate, and I remember so clearly how their faces looked—so much more relaxed and lighter after they heard the message that they would be okay and saw the numbers to back it up. They sat up straighter, and you could tell they could breathe deeper.

No matter what your situation is, it's important to get clear on the facts. This way, you can, first, calm your worries, and second—even if the numbers are as bad as you thought—get creative to do something about it. Now, at least you know for sure. Having the facts will help you get out of freeze mode.

This was the case with a mom who was in one of my courses. She was stressed out about money and kept saying she was broke. However, when we discussed specifics regarding her financial situation, it became clear she didn't know what her financial situation was or how much more she needed. She was too scared and embarrassed to put the numbers in a spreadsheet.

After discussing money shame and the impact of money stress, she was able to dive in and get all the info she needed about her financial situation. It turned out she needed to bring in about $800 more per month. You might think that that news was depressing, but the opposite was true. With a definite amount to work towards—call it a goal—she was able to start looking for more ways to bring in money. She immediately began to brainstorm about how to close the gap. Instead of feeling defeated, she felt empowered and relieved!

Another example is a single mom I spoke to many years ago; we'll call her Ashley. She came to me asking for help with her finances. She explained she was really stressed about money and that money was a major source of the fights with her teenage daughter.

Listening to her talk, I got the impression that she was struggling to make ends meet and thus was experiencing money stress—and that the stress was spilling over into her relationship with her daughter. She was in a panic, stressed to the max and felt she didn't have enough money to live comfortably.

Once we got to the numbers part with Ashley, she wrote them down, and we totalled them. Much to her surprise, and mine, it turned out she was a millionaire! Through her divorce several years prior, she had received equity in the house and a large sum of money, which she had invested. But none of this had registered in her brain yet. As a result, she lived in constant fear of running out of money.

The stress and worry disappeared once she had her financial situation laid out. Because she was now able to process the information, we could create a plan with her thinking brain on board.

With clarity about where she was financially, she could see more clearly how to move forward and create a better way to communicate with her daughter about money and expectations.

I'm sharing this story because it illustrates several things:

First, how we feel about money can be completely different from what actually is happening. In Ashley's case, she *felt* broke, yet she was anything but.

Second, you can experience money stress no matter how much money you have. Often, we think, "If only I had more money, then everything would be fine." But because these fears live in our subconscious, they can appear regardless of income level or net worth.

Finally, getting clear on your numbers is essential to managing money stress. Even if it had turned out that Ashley didn't have enough, at least then she would have known, and she could have created a plan to change the situation.

Clarity is your compass for charting a course forward, making informed decisions that pave the way for you to build the life you've always envisioned, free from financial stress or worry. Clarity will give you confidence and empowerment *no matter what* financial situation you uncover. Even if your financial situation turns out to not be great, at least now you know where you're at, and you can chart a new course.

Think of this process as an adventurous exploration!

## Your Turn

Let's clarify your financial situation and have you tap into the power of clarity. Even if you already have some sort of system, it's good to go through these steps.

I discovered how important that was many years ago. I was living life thinking I needed to bring in $2800 a month to be able to pay all my bills. That was my "bread-and-butter" number. I would think, "As long as I make $2800 a month, my bills are paid". And I wasn't just *thinking* that number; I was quite sure about it. I didn't mind numbers and had "sort of" figured it out. Or so I thought. Then, at one point, I was reading a book and the topic of expenses came up. I thought that would be a great time to start from scratch. I gathered all the info, and instead of guessing or estimating certain amounts, I looked them up on my bank account or the invoice. I was shocked to find out that my bread-and-butter number was, in fact, $3800! No wonder I sometimes had trouble paying the bills! Needless to say, it was a bit of a wake-up call, and I needed to increase my bread and butter minimum to at least $3800 a month.

Remember that I was also still running my "there's always just enough money, never more than I need" belief.

I now do this process with all my coaching clients and see the relief and confidence it brings, partly due to the clarity it provides but also because they've overcome a fear that held them back for so long. They might be reluctant initially, and sometimes, we have to take tiny baby steps. But the end result is always relief and pride.

## 4 Steps To Financial Clarity

(worksheet at the end of the chapter)

### Step 1: Setting the stage

First, we need to get into the right headspace to get a handle on our numbers. Remember your primitive brain? How it's lightning fast and has no capacity for language or math? And how it's run by emotions?

Creating space to breathe and calming our nervous system allows our thinking brain to be part of this process. Why is this so important? Because we need our thinking brain fully on board for the next few steps. Calming down your primitive brain is the key to success.

Also, become aware of your self-talk. What's going on in your mind? If certain thoughts take the wind out of your sails, write them down in your money journal and breathe. Be careful not to just push them away; it won't help, as they'll likely only get stronger. Instead, show yourself compassion and find out what you need in that moment to feel better. Remind yourself how much stronger you'll feel when you have all the numbers clearly laid out and can see exactly where you're at. No more doubt, no more wondering!

First, take some deep breaths, grab a lovely cup of tea or your preferred beverage, and clear the table so you have space. It's all about finding inner calm and setting the stage for this to be an enjoyable, exciting process.

## Step 2: Gather your statements

Next, to make sure you have easy access to the information you need, you'll want to collect your statements from the past month for the following:

- ☐ Your bank account(s)
- ☐ Credit card(s)
- ☐ Savings/investment account(s)
- ☐ Any other statement that shows details about income and expenses
- ☐ Receipts for anything you've paid for using cash (if you still have them)

Whether you use paper or digital PDF statements or have online access, it's entirely up to you. Go with whatever you prefer, whatever is most straightforward, and let's paint the most precise picture possible.

By bringing all this information together, you'll have everything at your fingertips and won't have to interrupt the fabulous flow you'll be in once you get started.

Don't worry! This is not something you'll have to do every month. We're gathering all the information *once* to get the picture. After you have done the exercise, you will have the clear picture you need, and I'll show you how to maintain it easily and effortlessly.

## Step 3: The magic of income tracking

The why of income tracking:

Do you know exactly how much money comes into your life each month, or are you guessing based on your paycheques? And if you're self-employed, are you basing what comes in on your significant sums, ignoring the small ones?

Here's what I've seen many times with my clients (and myself). By not keeping track of the money coming in (notice I'm not saying *income*), we don't know where we're at. Usually, only the large amounts register in our brains, and we ignore the smaller bits. But it all adds up.

For example, let's look at my coaching client, Judy. During one of our sessions, she expressed that she felt she was barely getting by and was struggling. "If only I could make more money," she sighed. She had a part-time job in retail and a home-based business.

I asked her what kind of income would make her heart sing. What would she need to earn to feel abundant and stop worrying?

"If I could make $4000 a month, I would be thrilled! But I only make about $2000 right now, so I would have to double my income and don't know how to do that," she said in exasperation. "Okay," I said, "Let's look at the numbers and see what is really happening."

The moment I hear people say "about this much" or "I think," it gives me a clue they are not tracking their income. We're always told to track our expenses and have a budget, so why would we track our income?

Remember that when we don't know something, our subconscious will fill in the gaps. It will make up all kinds of stories that, unfortunately, usually lean towards the negative. The little voice in our heads will assume the worst, and subsequently, our emotions will lean in that direction, too. At that point, we're feeling down and hopeless. We're stuck in financial quicksand. The uncertainty leaves us with unsteady footing, not in a place of strength.

So, one of the first things I do when working with people is to get clear on those numbers. It doesn't matter what they are— "good" or "bad"—if you don't know, you can't do anything about it.

And since you'll likely assume the situation is worse than it is, it might cause extra money stress, which we now know also might trigger dopamine-fuelled spending, compounding the stress.

So, when Judy started filling in the Income Tracking Spreadsheet, she pulled up bank and PayPal statements. This is where all her incoming money ended up. She filtered by *deposits* and entered the amounts on the spreadsheet. Much to her surprise, it added up to $3500. It turned out she had seen more clients in her business than she realized.

Remember how she said her dream income was $4000? She was only $500 away from that!

She was shocked and relieved to see this. It was like a weight had fallen from her shoulders. Now that she had clarity, she could think of solutions to create an extra $500 monthly. The dread, shame and worry had turned into hope, excitement and confidence.

She realized how important it was to continue tracking her income, so she always had the numbers to give her subconscious the correct information.

And in case you're wondering why she didn't know, or where that extra money had been going, we'll get to that in the following few chapters.

The how of income tracking:

Go to www.yourmoneywellness.com/book to download my Income Tracking Spreadsheet. As you'll see, it's super simple, and that's the whole point. Simplicity is what we want. I've had clients redo the spreadsheet and make it fancier, adding all kinds of lines and formulas. But then the principles of it get lost, and it doesn't have the same impact anymore. So, stick with this format and keep it simple.

Here is a sample of the sheet to download for this exercise:

| January | February | March | April | May | June | July | Aug | September | October | November | December |
|---------|----------|-------|-------|-----|------|------|-----|-----------|---------|----------|----------|
| $      | $       | $     | $     | $   | $    | $    | $   | $         | $       | $        | $        |
| $ 5,000.00 | $ 5,000.00 | $ 5,000.00 | $ 5,000.00 | $ 5,000.00 | $ 5,000.00 | $ 5,000.00 | $ 5,000.00 | $ 5,000.00 | $ 5,000.00 | $ 5,000.00 | $ 5,000.00 |

| TOTAL YTD | $ - |
|-----------|-----|

Once you have the spreadsheet, open up your online banking and filter transactions for deposits only. Every bank is different, but most have this option. If you can't filter, no worries. It just means a bit more scrolling. Alternatively, if you use statements, look at the credit column.

If you have money coming into different accounts, you'll want to do this for each account.

*Look for any and all money coming into your account(s) and mark it in the left column on the spreadsheet for that month.* In the right column, you can note the source (important for later when looking for patterns and where you put your time versus where your money is coming from).

If you're also receiving cash, it may be a bit harder to fill in those numbers for past months, but from now on, record *every bit of cash* you receive, no matter how small. Even if you find a quarter on the sidewalk, add it to the spreadsheet.

**And every time you add an amount to the sheet, celebrate it! Acknowledge it! Do a happy dance! Money is coming into your life, and you want to appreciate it, no matter what amount.**

Ultimately, this is about changing how you perceive money. A happy dance will help do exactly that!

If we only celebrate the more significant amounts, a part of our brain is still in *not enough* mode, as if 5 cents were not enough to celebrate. ("It has to be more; otherwise, I'm not going to pay attention to it.") The problem with that mindset is that it carries resistance with it. And judgment. And restrictions. None of which help with an abundance mindset. You either welcome money into your life, or you don't; it can't depend on the amount.

**You want to be ALL IN! And look for every opportunity to celebrate.** This will also help with your hormones, reducing cortisol, increasing serotonin and getting you out of your primitive brain, even if only for a moment.

The more we do this, the more we train our brain, the more we manage our stress, and the more we will look for reasons to celebrate.

Once you start income tracking, you will see what I mean.

**What do we NOT want?**

Too many details. We don't need to record which day it came in and do NOT want to add a whole section to track our expenses. That defeats the purpose of this exercise.

We do NOT want to track on paper either. It's best to do this using the spreadsheet, which automatically totals your amount each time. It doesn't have quite the same impact when you do this on paper.

What you focus on is what you get more of! It's about managing emotions, shifting to the positive, and getting clear on the facts: in this case, the income facts.

**What else happens when we use the Income Tracking Spreadsheet?**

1. Once you've used it for a while, it will help put things in perspective, especially for self-employed people. Sure, you may have a slow month or months, but maybe you've also had better-than-average months. By having an overview, you can see the whole picture, whereas if you didn't have the sheet and only looked at the slow month, you might feel defeated about the slow month.

2. Below the TOTAL line, you'll see another line with a number. Here, you can put your target income in the formula, and the spreadsheet will automatically calculate how close you are to your target. For self-employed/business owners, this will help you realize you're on track, way ahead or have a way to go until you reach your target.

By seeing the facts and taking the emotions down a few notches, your brain can move into problem-solving mode. Ask, "How can I bring in more money this month?" *How* is the key here. You're not panicking, thinking, "Oh no, there's not enough!" That shuts your brain down even more. Often, by just asking yourself the *how* question, you will come up with some great answers. And you will be on the lookout for opportunities. This is a significant shift away from a scarcity mindset.

3. Below the sheet, you'll see the year-to-date (YTD) total. This is so you know exactly where you're at for the year. No surprises at tax time. Speaking of tax time, this is NOT necessarily the sheet to bring to your accountant, as there might be several entries that are not part of your taxable income, like birthday gifts or money found on the sidewalk.

4. Look for patterns and learn from them. After using this sheet for many years, I can easily see patterns from year to year and month to month. It gives me such a boost to see how my income has doubled, tripled and quadrupled over time. The more I do this work, build my relationship with money and pay attention, the more my income goes up! I also see this with my clients, so I know it works! Quite often, the second or third month into the tracking, the income is already up from what it was. I can't wait for you to experience this for yourself as well!

## Benefits of Income Tracking:

✓ Often our emotions decide if we 'have enough', 'earn enough' etc. But now that you're tracking it, you can see the actual amount you're bringing in each month, and you're crystal clear. That clarity will help with the money stress. Even if the income isn't quite what you thought, or need, you now know exactly where you're at and can think of some steps to increase your income.

✓ We get a positive boost every time we celebrate money coming in.

✓ Throughout the day, you will now be looking for money, so you can add it to the tracking sheet, instead of expenses. Along the lines of "what you focus on is what you get more of", you'll be focussing more on ways to welcome money into your life.

✓ Smaller amounts usually don't register in our brain. But now, even the small amounts get acknowledged and added to the total. And it all adds up!

✓ If we get deposits into our personal accounts, where bills also get paid from, the money normally often gets used before we even notice it.

✓ By seeing the months side-by-side, you can put them in perspective: lower income months might normally have been stressful, but now that you see the bigger picture, you can put it in perspective. This will help manage your emotions and stress levels.

✓ You can start to see patterns: once you have used the form for a while, you'll be able to see patterns in your income. You can now also see where most of your money is coming from and then compare that with where you spend most of your time. It will allow you to pivot if needed.

## FAQ's:

- **What about refunds?** We only want to include "new" money, money that's new to us. Refunds consist of money we spent and are now getting back, so you don't want to include them even though they will appear on your bank account as a credit.

  Tax refunds are an exception to this, as it's not guaranteed you will get a refund. Even though it is money you "gave" to the government during the year, it's not certain you will get some of it back. So, if you like, you can include tax refunds in the spreadsheet.

- **I get paid by many clients a day. Do I mark them all separately?** If that is the case, it might not be practical to mark what each client paid you, as the column will get so long that it becomes cumbersome. Instead, total your amount for the day and add that amount to the income tracking sheet.

Many of my clients are therapists who use accounting software that gives them a monthly amount. However, waiting until you have the overview for the month is not recommended. You'll want to celebrate as often as possible, so recording money daily works best. Some of my clients estimate their daily amount and adjust it once their software shows them the monthly amount. That way, they've been able to celebrate each day and still have the correct amounts at the end of the month.

- **I am on salary. Why should I bother tracking? It's the same every payday.** Track it anyway, and do your happy dance! Remember, we're not just tracking income. We're tracking ALL money coming in. You might be surprised at what extra amounts show up. For example, a government payout or credit, birthday gifts or money found on the street. Yes, that happens too. You'll see!

- **I am in a relationship. Do we track together?** Yes, you can both add your incoming money to the same column. Or you can use the couple's tracker, where you each have two columns for the month, side-by-side.

For the tracking exercise, go back as far as possible, ideally to the beginning of the year. You don't have to do it all at once. Just see what works for you. The farther you go back, the faster you'll be able to see averages and patterns.

**And from now on, make sure you add money coming in right away and celebrate every single time!** Do a happy dance, even if you only get a dollar, because you want to welcome money like the friend it is, and not tell it or yourself it's not important or it's not enough.

Even though this is a straightforward exercise, when we turn celebrating money into a daily habit and celebrate like crazy, magical things happen! I know, it sounds a bit woo-woo, but who cares? It works. I can't wait for you to find out!

 Please make sure you share your experiences in the Money Wellness Community on Facebook.

## Step 4: Your money outflow

Now that you're clear on money coming in, let's look at the money going out.

Remember, breathe. It will all be okay!

On your Income Tracking Spreadsheet, you will see another tab named Cash Flow. Click on that to get the spreadsheet for this step.

There are several ways to complete the spreadsheet, depending on how comfortable you are with spreadsheets. I have found that some people see a spreadsheet and shut down. If that's you, and you are overwhelmed by spreadsheets, then download the worksheets first: each category is on a separate page, so you can work on one sheet at a time, make notes, scribbles, etc. Once you've completed the sheets, you can enter the totals into the spreadsheet.

Over the years, I've found that this in-between step makes the exercise more manageable if you don't like spreadsheets or numbers (yet).

Here are samples of the worksheets you can download (Appendix A in the downloadable workbook):

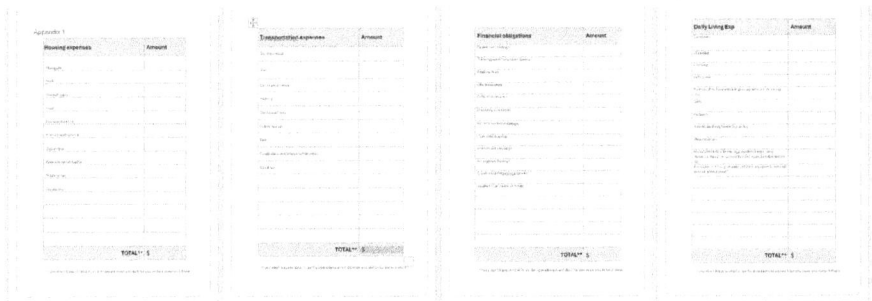

If you are comfortable with the spreadsheet, you can bypass the worksheets and enter the numbers directly. Below is a picture of what the spreadsheet looks like. You can find the full-size version in the same file as the Income Tracking, using the Cash Flow tab.

To get a crystal clear picture of your money outflow – your expenses – *use the tab called Cash Flow on the spreadsheet you downloaded for the Income tracking* at www.yourmoneywellness.com/book. That way, you can toggle between the two sheets easily.

| Family income/mo | Salary | | | | Monthly Expenses | | | |
|---|---|---|---|---|---|---|---|---|
| after tax or add tax payable as expense | Self-empl | | | | | | | |
| | Other | | | | **Housing expenses** | Amount | **Transp expenses** | Amount |
| | Total | $ - | | | Mortgage | | car insurance | |
| **Assets** | **Amount** | | | | Rent | | Gas | |
| Chequing Account | | | | | Power/Hydro | | Car maintenance | |
| Savings Account | | | | | Heat | | Parking | |
| RRSP | | | | | Home insurance | | Car Lease/ loan | |
| TFSA | | | | | Home maintenance | | Public transit | |
| RRIF | | | | | Cell phone | | Taxi | |
| Non-reg | | | | | Phone/internet/cable | | BCAA | |
| RDSP | | | | | Property tax | | | |
| Home value | | | | | Condo fees | | | |
| Other | | | | | | | | |
| | | | | | TOTAL | $ - | TOTAL | $ - |
| TOTAL | | | | | | | | |
| | | | | | **Financial obligations** | Amount | **Daily Living Exp** | Amount |
| **Insurance** | **Premium** | **Coverage** | **Type** | | RRSP | | Groceries | |
| Life | | | | | TFSA | | Cleaning | |
| Critical illness | | | | | Interest/fees | | Clothing | |
| Disability | | | | | Life Insurance | $ - | Eating out | |
| | | | | | Critical Illness Ins | $ - | Alcohol | |
| TOTAL | | 0 | | | Disability insurance | $ - | Gifts | |
| | | | | | Income tax installments | | Hobbies | |
| **Debt** | **Balance** | **Min. payment** | **Interest rate** | **Duration** | Gym membership | | Hair/Nails/Pedi/Man | |
| Mortgage | | | | | Investments Savings | | Memberships | |
| Line of Credit | | | | | Emergency Savings | | Weekly/monthly Trave | |
| Credit Card | | | | | Credit card min pmt | | Entertainment | |
| Credit Card | | | | | Student loan / LOC | | | |
| Student Loan | | | | | | | | |
| Car Loan | | | | | | | | |
| Other | | | | | | | | |
| | | | | | | | | |
| TOTAL | | $ - | | | TOTAL | $ - | TOTAL | $ - |

To get the numbers, grab your bank statement(s) and credit card statement(s) for one month (see step 2) and mark each withdrawal or payment on the spreadsheet in the corresponding category. I've prefilled some of the categories so you have a starting point. You can add more types of expenses if you have others in that category. You can also change the name of the pre-populated expense to better reflect your situation. Take your time doing this! And if you start to feel overwhelmed, stop, step away and take some deep breaths. Walk around, have some tea, or do something else until you feel up to returning to the exercise.

Do the same for your account balances, investments/ assets and debts until the spreadsheet reflects your complete financial picture.

Once you're done, congratulate yourself! You have clarity! Now, you can see exactly where you're at in one glance. You know how much money is coming in, how much is going out and where it's going.

## Clarity about your finances...

That's worth celebrating!

To get even more insight into your money outflow, you can ask yourself these questions:

- Compare the money coming in with the money going out. Is it more? Less? Same?

- What are the largest expenses, other than your rent or mortgage?

- Are you surprised by any of the numbers?

- Are there any expenses you want to or can change?

- If you bring in more money than you need for all the expenses each month, is that reflected in your bank account? For example, if your income is $5000 a month, and your expenses add up to $4200, do you have $800 left in your account each month? And if so, what do you do with it?

- If not, and you even have debt, it's usually a sign there's a fair bit of emotionally charged spending (dopamine). Not the end of the world. However, this will be a good time to go back to the emotions tied to the income and expenses, and work through the other exercises in the book. The Happy List will be especially important to fill out and follow.

Your financial journey is much like starting a road trip. To find your best route, you need to know the starting point. Later in the book, we'll work on finding your destination, or at least your next stop and target income.

Maybe the numbers are worse than you thought. That's okay. That's your starting point. At least now you have clarity and can start looking at ways to make changes. Whether it's creating more income or lowering your expenses, you can see what you need to do because you know where you're at.

However, chances are the numbers are not nearly as bad as you thought. If that's the case, take some time to let the numbers, and the reality, sink in!

How does that feel? Does it ease the anxiety and stress?

Often, once we have clarity, the stress falls away. We can breathe more deeply and relax. We can reach our thinking brain again and make sense of things. We can also access our creativity again and come up with some excellent ideas on how to make our situation *even better*.

There will be hope, energy and even excitement! With these things, we can change our money story and our relationship with money. Throughout this process, let's remember to celebrate our courage, commitment and every win, big or small. I'm cheering you on!

**Progress is more crucial than perfection!**

With each step forward, no matter how minor it may seem, you're pulling yourself out of the quicksand and flexing your financial muscles. Woo-hoo!

This process works on SO many levels. It's not *just* about the numbers. It's a truly holistic process.

One client came to me at her wits' end. She had trouble paying her bills, was in debt, and didn't know what to do anymore. She was reluctant to get her financial situation on paper, as she was scared to see how "bad" things were, and ashamed of her situation. Working through the shame and breaking down the numbers into small steps, she got her income and outflow all organized and documented in the end. And yes, her expenses were higher than her income, as she thought.

However, now she was able to walk through solutions with me. We found some money leaks, rearranged some expenses, and brainstormed ways to bring in more money quickly and easily. She was so happy at the end of this exercise! The relief she felt was palpable. And she was excited to implement some of the steps we had discussed.

By completing the spreadsheet, you've also laid the foundation for the Money Wellness Cash Flow system, which is a budgeting alternative. I always say that budgets don't work. (You can find the link for my video "Why Budgets Don't Work" on www.yourmoneywellness.com/book)

Let's just say budgets are tedious and don't work *with* your brain but against it. We're not walking calculators and cluttering our minds trying to keep track of how much we've spent in a category doesn't work.

The apps that exist to track your spending do offer insight into where your money went, but that's just it: by the time it shows in the app, the money is already gone. You've already spent it—and if it turns out that it was a dopamine-fuelled expense that wasn't in the plans, it's too late (unless you can return it).

These traditional ways put our relationship with money under stress, as they are tedious and, to most people, feel restrictive.

Is there a better way? Yes, there is! You can learn all about it in the Money Wellness Blueprint course. You can find more details and a discount code at www.yourmoneywellness.com/book.

## Your Turn

Using the steps from this chapter, complete the Income Tracking Spreadsheet, and the Cash Flow spreadsheet.

Remember, take as many breaks as you need. Be gentle with yourself! One step at a time, and you'll get there. You've got this!

# Chapter 6

# Hot Potato Spending

Now that you have more clarity about your money flow, let's have a closer look at a behaviour that often surfaces. I call it *hot potato spending*, which revolves around how we receive and spend money.

This pattern often emerges when someone suddenly gets a one-time or continuous influx of "extra" money, especially if they've felt scarcity for some time.

The hot potato spending concept ties together the other concepts we've explored thus far in the book: the influence of the primitive brain, dopamine, our beliefs about ourselves and money, and the impact of uncertainty.

Here's a typical scenario: money comes in, usually a more significant amount than we're used to or expected, and whoo.... We immediately spend it, as quickly as possible, just like we'd do if we had to catch a hot potato. The money doesn't get time to land.

We don't let the money sit for a minute, allow our brain to register that we have it and enjoy having it. We don't enjoy the feeling of being someone with that amount of money in our account. We just react and send it off to do something. It bounces right out of our account again.

Does this sound familiar at all?

It's important to note that hot potato spending doesn't necessarily mean you waste money or spend it on unnecessary items. You might use it to pay bills, reduce debt or make essential purchases.

The defining characteristic is the *sense of urgency*, often accompanied by a rush of excitement and anxiety. Dopamine plays a significant role in creating this frantic feeling.

We often see hot potato spending with tax refunds: you know the refund will come in, and it feels like extra or "free" money. Before the money even lands in your account, you may have already spent it in your mind. You might have already planned to book a trip, buy new clothes, pay off some debt or commit to certain purchases.

The marketing messages we around the time of year the tax refunds get paid out reinforces this behaviour, suggesting you should splurge on cars, trips or jewellery:

*"Getting your tax refund? Why not buy this new car? Book this trip! Get these beautiful earrings! You deserve it!"*

The people who create ad campaigns understand this concept too, and play right into it.

As mentioned, this behaviour doesn't always lead to frivolous spending; we might use the money for essential purposes. Nevertheless, the urgency and the dopamine rush are part of it.

The key component of hot potato spending is the *feeling and the urgency behind it.*

**It's the not letting it sink in that you have money and spending it right away that makes for hot potato spending.**

**The behaviour is unconscious and reactive.**

Dopamine will give you a feeling of reward and achievement once you've spent the money.

Sometimes, we don't even wait for the money to appear in our account. We may have already put it on our credit card, counting on paying it off once the money arrives.

Another example of hot potato spending can be seen in lottery winners. Statistics from the US show that a whopping 64-75% of the people who win large sums of money in the lottery end up in worse financial situations 3-5 years after their windfall.[5] This means only 25-37% of the people who win the lottery manage to hold on to their wealth.

They might treat the money as free or extra and part with it much more easily than they otherwise would. For instance, they might change their lifestyle significantly,

---

[5] https://www.ranker.com/list/why-most-lottery-winners-blow-through-their-money/nathan-gibson

make impulsive investments, buy things they have never been able to, or give it away to friends or relatives. None of this has to be a disaster, but when the primitive and emotional brains are in charge, impulsiveness and a sense of urgency follow.

In these cases, the lottery winnings are treated like one big hot potato!

I truly do see this type of spending happen at all income and wealth levels. The way it looks is different, and the consequences are different, but how it feels is the same.

## What's behind hot potato spending?

Often, hot potato spending can be traced back to a combination of dopamine, an old limiting belief, and the unfamiliarity of having that amount of money in your account. This strongly correlates to what we'll cover in the next chapter when we look at the *money thermostat*.

For some, hot potato spending is a response to years of feeling they didn't have enough money (keep in mind, *enough* is different for everyone). When money shows up, it's seen as an opportunity to catch up on delayed or desired expenses.

For others, it can be that we can't see ourselves as someone with that amount (whatever that amount is) in our bank account. Let's say your belief is "There's only just enough money" (or never quite enough). Or we (subconsciously) feel we don't deserve it. Then, receiving so-called *extra* money will feel strange and might trigger this type of spending.

It can also happen when we don't have a larger financial plan for ourselves. We might just pay bills as we go, not really sure how much money we have or need, and when the extra money comes in, it feels like a surplus, so we just spend it. We don't look ahead and don't think about setting money aside for a cushion, repairs, retirement or other things. We have a short-term vision.

Let's find out if you're familiar with hot potato spending, and if so, see what's behind it for you.

## Your Turn

Can you think of some examples in your life where you tossed the "hot potato"?

What was your self-talk in that moment?

What were you saying and feeling when this money came on your radar?

How did you feel once the money was out of your account?

Write down some instances you remember, then dive into them more deeply.

The insight will give us clues as to what can be done to cool down the hot potato and reduce our reactiveness.

## Cooling down the hot potato

To reduce hot potato spending, start by consciously welcoming money into your life *before* planning what to do with it.

Remember the "if money was a person" question I posed in the intro? How are you treating this money person when you're hot potato-ing? Are you slamming the door in their face, saying, "Oh, you're here, but I don't have space for you, so get out."?

How can you change your response and treat money as a good friend, welcoming it and inviting it in?

The **happy dance** that's part of the income tracking exercise will help. **Focus on the arrival of money and receiving it consciously** before doing anything else. This way, you intentionally welcome money and appreciate that it showed up for you.

**Allow the money to settle** in your account for a day or a week, resisting the urge to spend it immediately.

During this time, pay attention to your inner dialogue and self-talk, addressing any impulsive urges or feelings of unworthiness. What is the inner chatter about? Does it nudge you to do something with the money? Or maybe it's saying, "Who are you to have this money?" Or "Do something quickly before it's taken away," like my client Katie, in Chapter 4, believed after her parents and her brother took away her carefully saved money. Or if you feel like the money is "burning a hole in your pocket," ask yourself where the rush is coming from.

Whatever your version is, **breathe through that**. It's just fine for the money *and you* to sit there for a minute! You can also journal about how that feels and get more insights that way.

If the process feels uncomfortable, lean into it. There are some nuggets there for you to explore!

Become aware of what's going on for you.

Awareness is vital to cooling down your "potato."

Another way to prevent hot potato spending is to create a plan ahead of time for what you will do with extra money.

For example, you can make an agreement with yourself, such as this one:

Any time unexpected money comes in or my monthly earnings exceed X amount, I will move the extra money into (this separate account) for the cooling off and welcoming period.

And then I will take __% to treat myself, ___% to put away in my cushion account (emergency savings) and ___% to debt/retirement/car account. You decide on the percentages and the destinations.

Make sure you write this down somewhere so you can refer to it right away when you find yourself in a hot potato situation, and you don't have to make those decisions on the spot.

Note: the extra accounts are part of the Money Wellness Cash Flow system that I teach in my course, The Money

Wellness Blueprint, as part of handling day-to-day money in a way that works *with* your brain.

To recap the solutions to hot potato spending:

- **Welcome the money into your account.** I know it might feel silly, but give it a go! It's about bringing how you receive money to your conscious mind rather than your reactive subconscious.

- **Let the money sit as long as you can.** Don't use the money until you're calm and ready to consciously spend it or move it to a savings account. If you don't need to use it to pay bills or buy anything, move it into a separate account, to separate it from the day-to-day money. When our brain sees a large sum of money, no matter how disciplined we are, the temptation to spend it will be there. So, out of sight, out of mind works best here: open up a savings account and move it in there. Or if you already have an investment account and it's suitable for this money to go there, do that. Don't leave it in your chequing account, as it can trigger dopamine-fuelled spending.

  And listen to your inner chatter while the money is in your account. Notice what comes up for you. Discomfort with it still being there? Excitement? Restlessness? What thoughts and feelings do you experience?

## Create a plan:

- ✓ When I bring in more than $_____ in a month, I will use:

- ✓ \_\_\_\_\_% to treat myself – have fun with

- ✓ \_\_\_\_\_% to put towards my cushion account

- ✓ \_\_\_\_\_% to pay down my debt (if applicable)

- ✓ \_\_\_\_\_% to use for ...............................

You decide how you want to divide this up.

## Summary

Hot potato spending is a reactive way of spending money immediately after it arrives in your account or even as soon as you know it is on its way.

The underlying cause of this behaviour can be a limiting money belief, such as "I don't deserve." Or you might think, "I deserve this, so I'm gonna get what I want."

There is absolutely nothing wrong with spending money. The reactiveness and the rushed feeling behind the spending make this a not-so-helpful behaviour.

Being a good receiver is about receiving fully and consciously, with grace, intent, awareness and appreciation—feeling worthy of and embracing what you receive. You can receive money into your life without stress or anxiety and spend it with awareness, consciousness, alignment and purpose. When you're a good receiver, you are able to ask for what you're worth.

## WORKSHEET

Hot Potato Spending is the reactive and unconscious way to spend a larger-than-normal amount of money. This can be caused by being uncomfortable receiving the money, not feeling worthy, feeling that it's free money, feeling like it's a surplus and many other limiting beliefs. It's often driven by dopamine as well.

### Here are some steps to counter Hot Potato Spending:

- **Welcome money into your life.**

  record it on the income tracking spreadsheet, do a happy dance, and take a moment to appreciate money showing up for you

- **Let the money sit in your account for a while.**

  don't spend it right away, and don't use it to pay a bill right away. Let it sit, and be present to the fact that you have this money in your account. It's about getting used to seeing the new amount.

- **Write down what the chatter in your head is about the money.**

  This will give you an insight into the reasons for the hot potato spending, and the not-receiving well.

- **If you don't need that money to pay bills, move it into a separate account.**

  You can create a separate savings account for it.

- **Create a plan:**

  When I bring in more than $_____ in a month, I will use:

  - ____% to treat myself – have fun with
  - ____% to put towards my cushion account
  - ____% to pay down my debt (if applicable)
  - ____% to use for ...............................

  You decide how you want to divide this up.

Being a good receiver is about receiving fully and consciously, with grace, intent, awareness and appreciation—feeling worthy of and embracing what you receive. You can receive money into your life without stress or anxiety and spend it with awareness, consciousness, alignment and purpose.

# Chapter 7

# Your Money Thermostat

A concept closely related to hot potato spending is the *money thermostat*. I'm thrilled to introduce this concept to you, as understanding and reshaping your beliefs about it can tremendously impact your life. Both concepts revolve around our relationship with money and how it shows up in our lives.

In my experience, hot potato spending relates more closely to one-time or lump sum amounts, while the money thermostat pertains to longer-term financial changes, such as a pay raise. However, this is not a rigid distinction. The two concepts offer different perspectives on typical money behaviours.

So, what is the money thermostat all about?

Have you ever noticed that you often find yourself in a similar financial situation, with similar income or debt? Even if you get a raise, it seems like a year or so later, you still face the same issues, complaints or struggles with money or your living situation. It's as if nothing has changed, even though you may live in a nicer place or drive a better car. It's fascinating, isn't it? This could be your money thermostat in action.

To understand this concept better, let's look more closely at how a thermostat works. A thermostat is intended to keep the temperature in your home just right. We set it to a temperature we think will be comfortable, and when the room temperature falls below the set number of degrees, the heater comes on. When the room temperature exceeds the set number, the heater turns off. (In that case, we might open the windows to let some cool air in.)

Similarly, the money thermostat metaphorically keeps your financial life within a familiar zone—your comfort zone—even though *familiar* might not truly be comfortable. The thermostat's setting is determined by subconscious beliefs about yourself and money.

For instance, let's say you believe that life is a constant struggle and that you never seem to have enough money. And let's say you receive a raise, and life becomes more manageable. With the additional money coming in, you may initially feel a sense of relief, thinking you can breathe again and accomplish all these things you've wanted to do for so long. Your spending will likely increase, and you'll get things you've wanted or needed. Maybe you can even go on that long-awaited holiday!

But hold on a minute. That old tape of "Life is a struggle and I don't have enough money" still plays in your subconscious. Because this tape is running and impacting your actions and spending, you might find yourself right back where you started, *feeling* the same as you did before. It's as though you've unconsciously reaffirmed the belief that "life's a struggle, and I don't have enough money." Do you recognize that pattern in your relationship with money?

You might notice that you always, somehow, despite earning more or less, find yourself at a familiar financial point. Let's call this your *setpoint*. It's not too hot or cold, just right where you believe you should be. Again, I'm not saying this is where you *want* to be. Because it's subconscious, it just happens.

Our subconscious determines our decisions and actions, so we often end up in the same spot again and again, without even realizing it—until we start examining the situation, which is precisely what we'll do in this chapter.

## Your setpoint dictates your financial behaviour.

Your money thermostat works in the other direction as well. Let's say you're going through a rough patch and your income drops. What happens? Your internal money thermostat kicks in! You cut back on expenses, look for more affordable options to your usual purchases, work extra hours, or even start a side hustle. Before you know it, you've returned to your comfort zone, and all is well again.

When we hit the jackpot or get a raise, don't we all start living a bit (or a lot) more lavishly? We might splash out on gifts or vacations, or get that membership we've wanted for a long time. We might even move to a bigger place or get a nicer car.

And we'll likely have the justifications for it, too: "Yeah, but I needed a new car anyway because..." (fill in the blank).

We "open the windows" to let the extra money out. I know, the metaphor isn't perfect, but you get the idea. Despite the extra money, we often return to our old comfort zone sooner than expected.

Isn't that similar to how we handle money sometimes? We keep spending until our bank account tells us we've gone overboard and need to backtrack. All the while, we keep feeling the same familiar feelings we had before the money came in.

The money thermostat, driven by underlying beliefs, can keep us trapped in a cycle of hustle and spend, or boom and bust. It ensures our financial situation keeps us in our comfort zone, even if that zone is not ideal.

To be clear, just like with the hot potato spending, it's not that you can't or shouldn't upgrade your lifestyle or spend money! It's about the feeling behind it. It's about the discrepancy between what you believe and your bank account.

## Your Turn

### How do we change this?

Let's look at how to change this dynamic in combination with finding out where *your* setpoint is.

To do that, use the worksheet to write down your total income for the past five years. You can look at your tax returns to find your gross income *before* any taxes or expenses are deducted. Then, complete the worksheet and follow the steps.

See the worksheet on page 131.

After you have gathered the information for the worksheet, some what-if scenarios might come up.

## WHAT IF?

### What if your income drastically decreased at some point in the past five years, throwing off the average?

I often see this happen after life-changing events like divorce, which usually significantly impacts both income and mindset. I also see that the identity shift from *part of a couple* to *single* plays a significant role. One might stay stuck at the new "what's possible" financially, which becomes the new set point.

So, if you look back over the past five years and there's a significant change in income or lifestyle, that can throw the average off quite a bit. In that case, see what amount feels more accurate for you as your setpoint.

For example, after my divorce, I wasn't as confident in making big financial decisions anymore, as if I'd lost my foundation. This happened even though I was the breadwinner for most of the marriage and the one who looked after all the finances and found solutions when needed. My ex was not the stable one in our relationship. Yet here I was, feeling unsteady and scared to make financial decisions after the divorce. Luckily, this circumstance set me on the path of learning about money and eventually becoming a financial advisor. But looking back, I can still see how, after the divorce, I needed to get used to my identity as a single mom and sole breadwinner. And how it took me quite some time to work myself out of the new setpoint I had, based on "There's only just enough money to get by" or "There's not quite enough."  And "If I want to make a lot of money, I can't be a good mom." It varied between the three. That kept me stuck for many years until I learned what I'm writing about in this book.

**What if your income increased drastically during the past five years, but still have the same worries?**

If your income drastically increased at some point, it may take a while for your mindset to come along with it. You may still be "opening the windows" because you relate more to the lower setpoint. In that case, go back to the numbers. The steps you took in Chapter 5 will help with this.

In the Money Wellness Blueprint course, I also take people through getting clarity on their finances, which helps reinforce the new financial reality, and then create a new, comfortable flow around that. One that aligns with how the brain and hormones impact our relationship with money.

Money thermostat behaviour happens when we don't pay attention. It happens subconsciously. And the moment we are clear about our numbers, the behaviour is conscious, and we can lean into the new reality more each day and with each decision.

## Consciously pick a new setpoint!

What income most resonates with you? I'm going to assume you want to change your mindset and expand your comfort zone and that your desired income is higher than what it is now.

Ask yourself what income would feel great for you and why. What does that new amount mean to you? Make sure it *feels* achievable.

If your old setpoint is $50,000 a year, and you make your new set point $1,000,000 a year, that's likely too big a jump for your brain and mind to follow. It will likely trigger resistance in your brain because you haven't worked your way up to it. You haven't *warmed* yourself up to it. That $1,000,000 doesn't feel like you yet. It might sound great, but you might not have a connection with that number yet.

So, make sure you do smaller and steady steps. What's wrong with first leaning into $75,000, then $100,000, and keep bumping it up from there? Watch how you feel and listen to the inner chatter to figure out what works for you each time.

I've seen these big jumps happen often at motivational self-help weekends. Everyone gets tremendously excited while they're there; they see that everything is possible. At the end of the weekend, there's always some new resolution. And (been there, done that) they declare they will make a million bucks this year! Woo-hoo!

Like I said, been there... I was so excited about making a million bucks, but at the time, I was barely making $60,000, if that. So, throwing that million-dollar goal out there didn't really mean anything to me. I felt disconnected from it, like it was too far away, too big a leap. To part of me, it felt impossible. In the back of my mind, there were thoughts like "Whatever, that's not possible for me" and "Who are you to make a million bucks?". Even though my motivation might have been for the million bucks, some old beliefs and fears got triggered, and I had to work through those first.

So, for this exercise, choose a number that stretches your comfort zone yet still feels achievable and exciting. Your number will pull you forward and make you feel like, "Hell yeah, I can do this!" It will be an amount that you can connect to emotionally.

Now, take a moment to immerse yourself in that experience. Imagine being someone who makes, let's say, $100,000 a year (using our example). How would that make you feel? What would life be like? Focus less on the material possessions and more on the emotional and experiential aspects.

As you repeatedly and consistently focus on this feeling, you'll become more at ease with that amount. Over time, you'll reshape how you see yourself and transform your mindset until that setpoint feels comfortable. It will evolve, step by step, until it becomes your reality. You will grow, adapt and expand your comfort zone, all while standing confidently in your power with money, because you can welcome it with open arms.

I saw the money thermostat in action (together with a bit of hot potato spending) with a friend of mine. She is self-employed and has tried many different business opportunities and ways to create income, trying to find her groove, yet consistently struggling financially. At this time, she had found something that brought in more money—or at least it had for the past four months—and she was making quite a bit more than she was used to.

She then posted on social media about the new car she had bought and how happy she was. Fantastic! I was pleased for her, too. Just like hot potato spending, it's not that this was a wrong decision. Or that she didn't need a new car. But when we spoke a few months later, she shared with me that, with the car, she had added a $600 payment to her expenses and was feeling the same money stress as she did in the past.

The critical thing is that she bought the car and committed to the car payment before getting used to making the new amount. Her setpoint hadn't had a chance to change yet! By adding this payment to her expenses, she was well on her way to returning to her old familiar struggle to make ends meet.

When we look at an example like this, please do so without judgment. We all do the very best we can, and because none of us have been taught until now about the human side of money, we don't know any better.

In my friend's case, it could have been helpful for her to find out what the car payment would be and then set aside that amount for a few months. That way, not only would she build up a little nest egg, but she'd also get used to that money coming out of her account, and the new expense.

This strategy is another way to apply the money thermostat to your life and expenses: pretend you've already committed to the new rent, mortgage or car payment and set this money aside. Get used to that money coming out of your account for several months. Does it impact the overall flow? Does it trigger any old beliefs?

Once you get used to consistently setting aside the money, you will feel more comfortable with the increased expense and can confidently commit to it.

> Along with our personal comfort zone, there's also the comfort zone of who we like to hang out with. We tend to surround ourselves with people in a similar financial situation or with a similar lifestyle and income to us.
>
> Take a moment to reflect on this... Think of the five people you spend the most time within your circle. What are their lives like? What is their income? Chances are, they're very similar to yours.

## WORKSHEET:

### What's your setpoint?

To find out what income you are used to, look at your income for the past 5 years. Remember to include any bonus, tax refund, or unexpected amounts (if you can remember) ... it all counts!

1.  20_____: $_____

2.  20_____: $_____

3.  20_____: $_____

4.  20_____: $_____

5.  20_____: $_____

Total:  $_____ Divide this number by 5.

### My current setpoint is $_____

Do you see a pattern?

Remember that your current temperature represents your PAST beliefs, thinking, actions and mindset. To INCREASE this number, you'll transform your mindset to match the NEW setpoint amount you want to create.

Pick the new amount of money you want to welcome into your life. Make sure it's JUST OUTSIDE your comfort level, so it's a bit of a stretch but still feels possible.

**I'm ready for my NEW setpoint to be: $_____**

Your new setpoint should feel realistic, achiev-able and exciting!

This will bring out your determination and courage to find solutions to make this happen and reach this new goal.

Visualize the way your life at this new setpoint. How would you feel? And bring that feeling in to the present as often as possible.

## Summary

In this chapter, we explored the concept of the Money Thermostat. Our money thermostat will make sure our money coming in, and our lifestyle, stays within a certain range, which is our comfort zone. That doesn't mean it's comfortable, but it's what we're used to. And it's based on beliefs about ourselves and money.

In the setpoint exercise, you found out what the setpoint is for your money thermostat, and set a new one. By leaning into this new amount, and most importantly, stepping into what it would feel like to be someone who brings in that amount of money, and lives that lifestyle, it will gradually feel more familiar. With that comes a change in behaviour, expectations and mindset, which will allow for this new amount of money to come into your life.

# Chapter 8

# How do you Receive?

Have you ever had a friend hand you an incredibly thoughtful gift, and you're standing there, holding the box, and the first thing out of your mouth is, "Oh, you shouldn't have!" Or maybe you've found yourself saying, "That's too much!" a little too often. You know what I mean, right?

The same goes for compliments: someone tells you they love your clothes or hair, for example, and right away, we bounce back the compliment by downplaying it.

You immediately push back the gift or the compliment without receiving it fully. It often makes us uncomfortable, and we want to push it away.

These responses often spring from our deeper beliefs about worthiness and humility.

Have you ever noticed yourself doing that? What we could be doing instead is saying "Thank you!" and take it in. Zip it! No explanation, no excuses, no minimizing. Take it in and see what that feels like!

Let's explore further how we receive with an open heart and a compassionate, non-judgmental mindset.

**The first part of learning to receive well is observing how you receive.** We'll start this process by looking at something simple: how you react when someone compliments you.

How *do* you receive a compliment? Do you immediately bounce it back by diminishing it?

When someone says, "I love your dress!" do you reply with something like, "Oh, this old thing?" or "I've had this for such a long time," or "This? I got this on sale," instead of saying thank you? If that's you, you're certainly not alone.

Now think about the last time someone gave you a gift. Did you feel a bit uncomfortable and try to downplay it? Or did you wholeheartedly receive the gift and welcome it in?

## ACTION STEP:

What I'd like you to do for the next few weeks (or even better, from now on) when someone compliments you is say "Thank you!" and then zip it! Don't downplay or minimize the compliment.

I know it can be hard to do this, but you can do it.

Then, pay attention to your self-talk. What's the conversation you're having with yourself? It will get easier each time you say thank you, and you'll be able to let both the compliment and your gratitude sink in more

> .And yes, this has to do with money. There's a saying: "How you do one thing is how you do everything." We can transform that into "How you receive one thing is how you receive everything." This is where it starts!

The second part of receiving relates to the concept called **mental accounting**. Don't worry; it's not as complicated as it sounds!

This term, used in behavioural economics and psychology, describes our tendency to treat money differently according to subjective criteria. We categorize our money into different levels of importance based on its source, purpose or emotional significance, rather than seeing every dollar that comes in as equal to every other dollar.

For instance, have you ever noticed that we often spend tax refunds quickly because it feels like *extra* or *free* money? And perhaps that inherited money can feel heavy with responsibility or guilt? It's fascinating how our brain labels money differently depending on where it comes from.

There might even be anger or resentment attached to the source of the money.

This is what a client of mine experienced. After a car accident, Rose "received" a large sum of money as a payout from an insurance company. But the process of getting that payout was so physically and emotionally gruelling and infuriating that those emotions ended up tied to the money she got. All the anger, feelings of betrayal and frustration showed up as the money arrived in her account. So, instead of enjoying the money and being relieved to have it, she ended up spending it with anger attached, still holding the vision of how she was treated as she handled the money. With this in mind, it is no surprise that the money was gone quickly. She explained to me how she was kind of relieved once the money was gone and was quite happy to start from scratch, which is where she was when we met.

Or let's say you win a decent amount of money in the lottery. You really need to get your car repaired and catch up on your retirement savings, but since this money feels like a treat, you decide to splurge and use it to go on holiday without much consideration for the car or retirement. It doesn't even really come up as a possibility. Why would you spend this free money on something so boring? So you spend the money on your trip, and off you go. You'll pay for the car and your retirement savings from the money you'll earn.

You may notice that mental accounting ties into hot potato spending and the money thermostat. In a way, mental accounting can be an underlying factor for the other two concepts.

Our "mental accountant" decides what money sources we'll use for hot potato spending. It's not a conscious decision; nonetheless, it happens.

Another way I see mental accounting show up is with cash on hand versus money in your bank account. People who get paid in cash have often mentioned this to me.

For example, if you work in the hospitality industry and get paid cash tips, that money often ends up in your pocket and gets spent without it even registering in your brain or bank account. This is why the income tracking exercise in Chapter 5 is so important: to make it land consciously and become part of your money as a whole, rather than being separate because it's labelled differently.

That brings us to how we can deal with mental accounting. Our brains are wired to make distinctions and label things, so we can't just turn it off. But we can put systems in place to be more aware of and manage the process more helpfully.

Starting with that awareness, look at all the money that comes into your life right now. Where does it come from? How does it make you feel? And most importantly, how do you receive it? What thoughts and feelings are attached to it? Does it register at all that money is coming in?

If you have a regular salary, you might notice you don't even pay attention to it coming in. It's just there; you use it to pay your bills and live. Not that exciting, right?

Yet how would it go if you received the gift from your friend the same way you received your salary? Pretty awkward, I'd bet!

At the end of the chapter or on your worksheet, you can write down the sources of money coming into your life in the left column and how you feel about it in the right column.

Contrary to popular belief, receiving isn't always easy; it can trigger fear when tied to the worry that "Now I owe someone something, and in the past, that has caused nothing but trouble." This is often a trauma response, and would require more extensive processing. But at least having the awareness of this is already a big step forward.

Regardless of your feelings about receiving, it's essential not to simply tell yourself to cheer up and move on. Instead, take the time to acknowledge those emotions; they exist to keep you safe. *After* you acknowledge your feelings, you can unpack the reason behind them and use your insight to find a way to shift how you feel.

## Your Turn

Before we dive in, let's see where you are now. This exercise will help you clarify how you feel about the different sources of money in your life.

Download the worksheet (www.yourmoneywellness.com/book), use the sheet at the end of the chapter, or use your money journal for this step.

On your Income Tracking Spreadsheet, you can identify the different sources of income. Put those in the boxes on the left. Then, for each source, in the column on the right, write down how you truly feel when this money arrives. Notice if there are differences between each source and if the emotion affects how you spend the money.

As always, look at this with no judgment. You're exploring what's happening to see if it still works for you. That's all. **Awareness is power!** And with your newfound awareness, you can now consciously change how you receive money each time it comes in.

## Summary

In this chapter, we focused on how you receive money. While receiving ties into the hot potato spending and money thermostat concepts, we looked at the emotions tied to money coming from different sources in this chapter. Mental accounting describes the idea that we may spend money differently depending on the feeling we associate with it.

By becoming aware of what emotion is tied to money from each source, we can start to recognize if we spend money from different sources differently.

Your awareness will help shift how you feel. You can also journal about this to work through your feelings.

The next time you receive money from a particular source, see if you can separate the source from the money and receive the money with gratitude and excitement.

## Worksheet:

Write down, or draw an image of, each source of money that comes into your life, as well as how you feel about it. What emotion is attached to the source of the money, if any? (To find the different sources of money, you can use the income tracking worksheet, or your bank statements/online banking platform.)

| SOURCE | EMOTION |
|---|---|
|  |  |
|  |  |
|  |  |
|  |  |
|  |  |
|  |  |

### Awareness is power!

With your newfound awareness, you can now consciously change how you receive money each time it comes in.

# Chapter 9

# Aligned Spending

When you read the title of this chapter, you may have thought to yourself, "What is she talking about? I don't have any problems with spending money. I love it!" However, there's more to spending than just handing over cash or tapping your card. Sometimes, we spend money from a subconscious or disconnected place, which this chapter will explore.

Much of the information we've covered thus far will be relevant to this chapter, for example, hot potato spending and dopamine-fuelled spending. This brings us to...

## The emotional side of spending

What often happens is that we *feel* a certain way about the money in our lives and transfer our feelings onto our spending. This is similar to what we discussed in the previous chapter about mental accounting in chapter 8.

For example, if you feel scared there's not enough money, you won't spend it with ease. You'll be so aware of *feeling* there's not enough that when you hand over the money or tap your card to purchase something, you'll do so with great reluctance. There'll be no ease and flow, and you won't end up receiving the item or service wholeheartedly.

That's why receiving encompasses spending. Spending is receiving. Think about that for a second.

## Spending is receiving!

It is an exchange. Money for a product or a service. You give the money; you receive something in return.

As you did in the chapter about receiving, ask yourself how open you are to spending and receiving something in return.

## Do you appreciate what you were able to buy?
## Do you feel worthy of it?
## Do you receive it fully?

Or do you feel awkward about receiving it?

Do you feel resentful? "Why did I have to spend money on this?"

Or maybe, "That was so expensive! Why didn't I get more for my money?"

If your subconscious belief is more along the lines of the last few sentences, then you're still saying:

**"It's not good enough."**
**"There's not enough."**
**"I don't deserve."**

So many of us walk around with a sense of "I'm not good enough" or "There's not enough", that it seems normal. This *not enough* can quickly turn into anger and frustration. When that happens, we might think, "Whatever.... It's not going to work anyway, so I might as well buy this," and we spend money on things we don't need, which don't fulfil us either.

It is similar to what can happen if we have a strong (negative) emotion attached to the source of the funds, like Rose in Chapter 8 did. She was so mad about how the insurance payout process had gone that she projected that anger onto the money and spent it with that same emotion. It wasn't fulfilling her. Heck, she wasn't even getting dopamine out of it all. She ended up just feeling resentful towards the things she had bought.

## Your turn

To become an aligned spender, self-care, awareness, and clarity will all come into play.

A great start is to do the "How do I receive?" exercise from the previous chapter, only this time do it for spending: put the expenses in the left column and how you feel about them in the right column. (I've put the exercise at the end of this chapter again.)

Once you've done that, you can look inward to see where the emotions are coming from and how you can shift your responses. Ask yourself what you *need* to feel better about spending money on that particular item, especially if it's a recurring, necessary expense.

It's also important to address *alignment*.

My take on *alignment* is matching your thoughts, emotions and actions, making sure they are all pointed in the same direction.

The example I often use is about cake. Let's say someone at a dinner party orders some lovely chocolate cake for dessert. But while they take a bite, they say, "I really shouldn't."

That is the perfect example of not being aligned. You're doing one thing while saying or feeling the opposite. "I shouldn't" and "I can't" are common thoughts here.

In this case, alignment would be to eat it, enjoy it, and zip it. No excuses or saying anything to the contrary. Or don't order it, don't eat it and feel good about sticking to your eating plan.

Both ways show alignment, and work well.

And the worst you can do is say one thing and do another.

Based on everything you've read so far, I recommend the following steps for aligned spending:

## 1. Ask yourself first: Is it a HELL YES?

Hell Yes is the best and quickest way to feel if you're aligned or not.

## 2. In principle, if it's not a Hell Yes, it's NO!

Or...if it's a Maybe, you can find out why it's not quite a Hell Yes. What's missing? What would make it a Hell Yes? If it's not a Hell Yes, why would you buy it? Is there a fear behind it? Or a sense of lack? Powerlessness? Urgency?

Marketers are experts at getting that sense of urgency across. BUY NOW, before it's too late! Before it runs out! Before this takes off! Messages like this are designed to bypass our logic and speak directly to our emotions. The fear of missing out is real. The urgency triggers more dopamine as well. More about that in a minute.

If it's an expense you must pay, like insurance, rent/mortgage, or even a parking ticket, is there a way you can find a positive in spending the money? Is there a way you can pivot and see the situation from a different perspective?

For example, with rent/mortgage, can you shift towards appreciation for having a place to live? Can you appreciate the insurance that ensures you can take care of your kids financially, no matter what happens? Can you even appreciate parking tickets?

When I got a parking ticket a few years ago, my first reaction was annoyance, and then I kicked myself for not seeing the meter. After that, I reminded myself that at least the money I'd pay for the ticket would be supporting the city with maintenance and road-building. That realization made me feel great, and I was able to pay for the ticket while feeling good about it. Whatever it takes to be able to pivot! Even if the pivot is not entirely accurate. Honestly, I don't even know if the money from parking tickets is used for road maintenance. But it doesn't matter. It made me feel better about the ticket, and it mattered that I didn't pay it until I felt good about it.

Play around with alignment and pivoting and see if you notice a difference. And then do what feels best for you! And if it takes an extra few hours, days or even a week before you can buy this item or pay that bill, so be it. Of course, if there's a deadline or due date, you'll want to work faster on your pivoting, but you get the idea.

Don't buy or pay until you feel good about it, or it's a Hell Yes!

**A little side note about gratitude versus appreciation:**

Notice I'm not talking about gratitude much in this book.

In my opinion, gratitude often has a bit of a heavy feeling to it. For example, "I'm grateful to have a roof over my head." It's too easy for someone to say that and have a bit of a defeatist or negative feeling creep in, along the lines of "At least I have a roof over my head and don't live on the street." It reminds you of the negative, and it feels a bit off.

When you say, "I appreciate having a roof over my head," do you sense you automatically want to put your hands on your heart and take a deep breath?

Do you sense that you can wholeheartedly say, "YES, I do appreciate that?"

In my opinion, appreciation is "cleaner" than gratitude.

If you find the typical gratitude exercises work for you and make you feel better, fantastic! Keep doing them. If not, notice what happens when you shift to appreciation!

## 3. Receive what you've bought fully and consciously.

Celebrate, enjoy and appreciate what you receive in return for your money.

Remember, spending is receiving!

Returning to the saying, "How you do one thing is how you do everything," it also translates into "How you receive one thing is how you receive everything."

In Chapter 8 about receiving, we talked about receiving compliments by saying thank you and then being quiet. No chatter, no minimizing it. Just say "Thank you!" and then zip it!

Same with a gift or a raise. "Thank you!"

Connecting this to spending, the next time you buy something in the store, take an extra few seconds to be conscious of paying, sending a quick internal message of appreciation: "I appreciate having the money to bring this item into my life... or... "buy this service." Or something along those lines.

Then, when the item is handed over, don't just grab it and walk away. Please take a minute to let it land, become conscious of it, and thank the sales clerk, server or whomever. Become aware of the exchange that just took place.

Let's not forget about dopamine.

We already touched on the impact of dopamine on our spending in Chapter 3. We looked at how we get dopamine when we buy certain things, especially when they are on sale. Dopamine gives us a natural high — a feeling of reward, of having achieved something. You now also know that since it doesn't last very long, we can get caught up in a vicious cycle or roller coaster. The dopamine makes us feel great, then it drops off, and we might feel depressed and look for another way to get a boost (go shopping again). We get more dopamine... and so on.

When dopamine fuels our urge to buy something, it is not a conscious process, as we can only focus on the shiny thing we just "have to have" because "it's going to be so great once I buy it."

Most likely, we won't be aligned either, as a contradictory feeling may fuel the spending: "I feel crappy and want to feel better, so I will treat myself to this." In this state, our spending is driven by a feeling of lack or the thought, "I need this so I can feel better... because I'm not feeling great right now." Do you feel the duality in this self-talk?

To direct the need for and impact of dopamine, you can return to the Happy List from Chapter 3. This list will help you manage your stress levels differently, so you don't depend on shopping or spending money to feel good.

Get more awareness about *why* you spend. What was the emotion you felt before buying that item or service? What went through your mind before you made that decision?

Please remember that I'm not saying not to spend or that it's bad to spend. Money is a wonderful tool to help us create the life we want! And money is on our side if and when we allow it.

We just want to check into where we're at *before* we spend and be aligned.

## WORKSHEET

Put the expenses in the left column and how you feel about them in the right column. (I've put the exercise at the end of this chapter again.

| SOURCE | EMOTION |
| --- | --- |
|  |  |
|  |  |
|  |  |
|  |  |
|  |  |
|  |  |

## Steps to Aligned Spending:

1. Is it a Hell Yes?

2. If not, what else is needed to make it a Hell Yes?

3. When you receive the item or service you have bought, take a minute to consciously receive it into your life, with appreciation.

# Summary

In this chapter, we explored the emotional side of spending and how spending is closely tied to receiving.

Spending is receiving!

Every time we spend money, we receive something in return.

The art of receiving happens beautifully when you...

- Spend consciously
  - o Instead of paying with a card, try using cash for a few months to get more up close and personal with money again.
- Spend in alignment
  - o Look for the HELL YES! If it's not a Hell Yes, it's a NO. So, either don't buy it or pivot into being able to spend the money, even if it's a routine payment.

# Chapter 10

# It's Safe to Have Money

I often translate the words *emotional side of money* into *mindset*. Although the word mindset is used in all kinds of ways these days, even overused, it's a bit easier to use as a reference sometimes. I see our mindset as the lens through which we view money, spending, receiving and our worthiness.

We improve our relationship with money by working on our mindset, including recognizing our emotions, triggers, stressors, limiting beliefs, and spending and saving habits. As a result, we find ease with money and see money as our friend.

Think of our capacity to hold money, wellness and abundance as a receiving bowl. Limiting beliefs and emotional hardwiring are significant causes of cracks in our receiving bowl, causing leaks and impacting our capacity to hold and tend to money.

If we have a leaky bowl, we might still be able to take action, like start a new business, sell a house, take on a new client, and bring money in. However, it will be like pouring water into the leaky bowl without fixing the holes (adjusting your mindset, emotions and sense of worthiness). The money won't stick around; it will flow out without you having control. When that happens, you feel powerless: you're working so hard, doing all these things, and yet you're no further ahead. How frustrating!

Money flowing out without us realizing is often why people get stuck in the "If you want to have more money, you have to work harder" mindset.

I wholeheartedly say NO to this. Working harder *while feeling like you don't have enough* or can't get ahead will just cause more stress and worry, not ease and flow.

In Chapter 3, about money and our hormones, you saw the impact of stress on our finances. We might start to depend on dopamine because we feel crappy and stressed out and spend money in areas that don't help us at all.

You've probably heard the saying, "Don't work harder, work smarter," too. This is better than "If you want to make more money, you have to work harder," for sure. But to work smarter, you have to access your thinking brain. That's where the logic, common sense, language and executive functions live.

From Chapter 2, "Money and the Brain," you learned that if we're stressed, the primitive brain, with its lightning-fast responses, takes over, and the thinking brain is sidelined until we calm down. So, "Work smarter, not harder" only works if we can access the thinking brain and make sense of things.

This is why I say, "**Work less, make more.**"

I know it's kind of cheeky. But think about it: when we work less, we have time for self-care, don't rush around, don't panic about everything we have to do, and our brain gets a chance to work at 100% capacity. We have time to be proactive rather than reactive.

Then, we can return to the "smarter" part of the previous saying. We also get more in touch with our creativity and come up with brilliant ideas while relaxing.

Years ago, when I started this work, I lived by the beach for a while and was shocked to see how well this worked. Every morning, my dog Scooter and I would go for a walk, and of course, we'd walk on the beach. We'd climb over rocks and look for seashells. Well, at least I did. Scooter would look for fishy things to eat, of course.

All the while, I'd hear the waves and feel the wind in my face. It was such a blissful time! By the time we got home, most of the morning would have passed.

Initially, I felt guilty for having "wasted" the whole morning, but I quickly realized how important this time was for me. I came up with the most fantastic ideas and solutions while walking. And, more often than not, I'd come home to emails from potential new clients and other great income-producing possibilities.

That's when it clicked for me: that time on the beach was my self-care time. It was a time for my brain to relax, my thinking brain to catch up, my emotions to settle, and for me to tap into my creative side.

When I finally relaxed, the hard shell of tension that had been around me cracked. Each day, each walk, that shell started to disappear more, and I could emerge as myself—the me who was not caught up in the rat race or worried about money—the me who knows fully that money shows up when I'm open to it. That year, living by the beach, my income quadrupled while working less and doing the same work I had been doing for a long time. Effectively, the only significant change was the walks along the beach (and me not booking any clients until after 11 a.m.).

I also slowly started to repair my receiving bowl, using the same exercises I'm showing you in this book. Doing the exercises reminded me of the powerful connection between our body, mind and money.

You might think, "Well, easy for her to say! I don't live by the beach," or "I can't afford to do that."

That's why I wrote this book! Because I know that by doing the work we covered here, you too will "fix your bowl" and be able to hold the space for money. You will be comfortable letting money flow in and not get rid of it immediately. And if you do spend money, you will do so with awareness and appreciation.

## Reframing

The final tool I want to offer you is something I find extremely helpful when coaching my clients. The tool consists of two sentence starters that will make a world of difference.

When you are bumping into some of our limiting beliefs, these sentence starters can make a big difference in shifting that. For them to work, it's important to play around with the words until you find the ones that feel best. This is best explained by first going into how it doesn't work.

Often, when we have a certain limiting belief, it's recommended to counter that by repeating the opposite of that belief many times, so we train ourselves into this new belief.

For example, if our deep belief is "I'm not worthy of money" or "I'm not good enough," and we start saying "I'm worthy" or "I am good enough." However, this is a direct contradiction of what's in our subconscious. That old belief is so engrained in our brain, like a well-worn path, that it takes a lot of energy to override the old belief and replace it with the new one. Aside from the energy it takes, what I find with regard to money beliefs in particular is that it simply reinforces the old belief more, instead of shifting to the new one.

When you say something directly opposite of an engrained pathway, you activate the old belief every time you say the new sentence. You can check this by noticing how you feel when you say one of the sentences above. Likely, it's too big a leap, emotionally speaking. Your brain might say, "Yeah, dream on," or "That's never gonna happen," or "Yeah, I really need that money because I don't know how I'm going to pay my bills right now."

Even repeating it over and over won't necessarily make the statement feel any better. It's a bit like picking at a scab. You keep reminding yourself of what isn't.

Similarly, by saying, "I am making a million dollars this year," or something along those lines, while you're barely scraping by, you're reinforcing the feeling that you don't have that million dollars! It reminds you of scarcity, not abundance.

Instead, I have found that using the following sentence starters is a way to get around all this. There's something about these sentence starters that speaks directly to the primitive brain and calms it down. There's no arguing or forcing your brain. It's more of an easy flow.

At the end of the sentence, you'll want to be in a place where you think, "Yeah, I am!" or some other version of that, seeing what you just said as possible and true. So, it's crucial to find the correct words.

When I have clients say these sentences we come up with, most of them immediately take a deep breath and smile. The sense of calm and relief is palpable right away.

Best of all, with the new sentence, there's no arguing with the old belief. These words access a belief we can embrace directly. Even more importantly, they make us feel better right away.

So, what are these magical sentence starters?

The first one is **IT IS SAFE FOR ME TO...**

From all the coaching clients, I've learned these often hit home the most:

*It is safe for me to have money.*

*It is safe for me to have more than enough money.*

*It is safe for me to talk about money.*

*It is safe for me to stop struggling.*

*It is safe for me to be successful.*

*It is safe for me to be seen.*

To figure out how to finish your sentence, you'll want to look at the notes you took while reading this book and check in with yourself to see what keeps you stuck regarding money. Then, find the sentence that speaks to that the most and that feels true to you.

Do some brainstorming: write down all the words you come up with so you can try them out and tweak them. You know you've found the right one when it really resonates with you. Often, my clients cry or choke up when we've found the words they need to hear. That's when you know you've got it!

Once you find the sentence that gives you that sense of peace, ease or joy, repeat it as many times a day as possible. Because every time you do, it draws out the sense that all is well, and that's precisely what we want! That's being in alignment. That's being without resistance. And ultimately, that's a whole step closer to a great relationship with money.

I feel that introducing the word *safe* stops the mind chatter and is the most significant of all the words in the sentence. Connecting the *safe* to money reminds you that money is not a scary thing you have no control over. It reminds you that you can be safe *and* look at money. There is no need to put your head in the sand anymore or run any old patterns keeping you where you are now.

The other sentence starter that works extremely well is:

## I GIVE MYSELF PERMISSION TO...

Some examples of this that have proven to be very powerful are:

*I give myself permission to stop struggling.*

*I give myself permission to be wildly successful.*

*I give myself permission to be debt-free.*

*I give myself permission to stop stressing about money.*

*I give myself permission to relax and have fun.*

*I give myself permission to get organized.*

Again, brainstorm and find what you need to give yourself permission for and notice how it feels to say the sentence. You have the correct wording if you choke up, get goosebumps, get emotional, or just *know*. Repeat your sentence many times a day. Or say it when you're paying bills, having a difficult money conversation, or asking for a raise. Recall the *feeling* of your sentence each time you say it.

In a way, that's the feeling of alignment. That's you honouring yourself and being on the same page with who you are meant to be. And that *feeling* is what will change your decisions, how you show up for people and, ultimately, it will change your relationship with money and your life.

I know, I know, it's a big statement to make. And I feel confident making it, as I've seen this work every single time I have used this with a client. And, of course, I use it myself.

Here are some examples: (Please understand these are only summaries. There's much more to all of this! However, I wanted to get the essence across to give you a better idea of how these sentence starters can work.)

## Client Example 1

One client had always been told by her family that she was terrible with money. As a result, she avoided having money for most of her life. She lived paycheque to paycheque and had debt, too. She had a deep sense of being "irresponsible" and "bad" with money, just like her family had told her she was. Even as she sat in my office, her shoulders would be hunched over; she didn't radiate any confidence at all. There was lots of shame and self-loathing going on, unfortunately.

Of course, we did all kinds of work to help bring awareness to and shift her old patterns. As I introduced these sentence starters and brainstormed how to finish them, the sentences that had the most significant impact on her were "It is safe for me to have money" and "I give myself permission to take good care of money." Saying these things out loud gave her a sense of "Yeah, I *can* do this." And, interestingly enough, she immediately sat up straighter. No more hunching over.

As she took these sentences into her daily life, repeating them and feeling the impact, she turned around her negative self-talk and self-image. She managed to get out of debt and increase her income pretty soon after. She also felt much more confident about herself and her abilities. She started believing in herself again, which was a fantastic shift to see!

## Client Example 2

Another client had a strong belief or imprint of "I don't matter" and "I shouldn't be here" because of things that had happened in her past. Her mom had passed away when she was young, and her dad remarried soon after. My client had interpreted some things that happened during that time as "I don't matter."

As a result, she was quite insecure and felt that she needed permission from others to do anything. She also avoided everything to do with money, since it seemed too scary and something she thought she'd mess up anyway. Subconsciously, her self-talk related to money was "I can't do this," "I need someone to help me with this," and "I'm not good enough."

Working with her on her money story and beliefs, her confidence and ability to stand up for herself grew immensely. As a result, she opened the business she really wanted to start. When she felt she had plateaued a bit after her business grew faster than expected, we pulled in the sentence starters.

The ones that worked best for her were "It is safe for me to be seen" and "I give myself permission to be successful" (*wildly successful* felt too much for her then, so we kept it for later). As a result, she showed up as an empowered entrepreneur in business meetings, closed new contracts and reached out to bigger organizations (that she had previously avoided), thereby expanding the reach of her business and securing future income.

## Client Example 3

Another client grew up with a mom who always said, "Only the very best is good enough for us." She had translated that into "I have to be the best" and, on the flip side, "I'm not good enough." This made her doubt what she wanted to do moving forward. And she hadn't applied her skills and knowledge. She took course after course and got many certifications without ever really applying what she learned in business or work. No matter how much she learned, she never thought she was good enough; she kept jumping to the next course or accreditation program.

When we did this exercise to determine which words would have the most significant impact, she suddenly said, "It is safe to be ME!" and immediately teared up. All those years, she had tried so hard to please her mom by being the best, pushing herself all the time and getting more degrees to prove her worth—so much so that she didn't feel there was room to be who she really was.

In the following months, she visibly relaxed, stood taller with her shoulders back, and had conversations with people in her life that she had avoided up until then. She applied her vast knowledge, created a business and started allowing money to come in.

## Client Example 4

Another one of my clients had a powerful hot potato spending reflex. Any time money came in, she spent it straight away. In fact, even before it had come in, she had already "spent" it by committing to certain purchases that weren't aligned with what she wanted in life. (Even if they had been aligned, the money wouldn't have had a chance to land, so it's still in hot potato territory).

In working with her, we covered many things that contributed to this reactionary spending, tracing them back to her childhood in an abusive household. There was a hefty dose of "I don't deserve to be here." The spending became her (subconscious) way of proving to the world she deserved to be here.

The sentence starters that worked best for her were "It is safe for me to have money" and "I give myself permission to be seen." As she worked with those, not only did her reactionary hot potato spending drop and her stress levels go way down so she could relax more, but more money also started to flow into her life, and her income increased significantly! It was like money now knew it would be appreciated and cared for.

\*\*\*\*\*

I hope some of these examples have given you an idea you can use for yourself on your money journey. And, of course, remember that these examples were heavily edited and shortened. It's a process with many facets.

## Your turn

Try it out yourself! If you don't feel that kind of relief or release, keep brainstorming and trying new words. You will know when you have found the right ones!

When you've got your sentence, write it on paper, on a card, or even save it as a screensaver. That way, you'll see it many times a day. And each time you repeat the sentence, your body will be reminded how good it feels to be safe.

It doesn't matter what your financial situation is at the moment. Whether you live from paycheque to paycheque or already have a fantastic income and lifestyle, if you feel better, you will do better.

Returning to our leaky receiving bowl metaphor, by reminding yourself you're safe or giving yourself permission to do or be something, a weight is lifted off you, and a sense of relief can flow in. This will start closing the leaks in your receiving bowl so money can flow in and stay in.

From there, the steps to happiness aren't far off. Along with happiness, a sense of ease, joy and appreciation follow suit. Add money to that mix, and you have all the ingredients to live life on your terms, fully supported by money!

One more thing to mention: I fully acknowledge that if you currently live in a precarious financial situation, this may be a significant shift, so *do what you can*. Start small. You don't have to go from zero to a hundred in a split second. Each little shift, extra breath, and slight drop in stress levels help your brain and body get into a calmer space so you can manage better and think more logically and creatively. And then, even if you can only think of tiny creative solutions to improve your situation, that's already 1000% better than any status quo. Don't give up hope if it doesn't work right away! Show yourself the same compassion as a friend in a similar situation.

## WORKSHEET: Reframing

Based on your core stresses around money, complete the following sentence starters.

Find the sentence that grabs you, and then feel that subtle shift in your shoulders, back, belly, or breathing. You'll feel the impulse to take a deep breath, and suddenly, the fear or stress you felt won't seem so daunting anymore. That's when you'll know you've found the right words to finish the sentence.

## It is safe for me to ....

- ✓ _____
- ✓ _____
- ✓ _____
- ✓ _____
- ✓ _____
- ✓ _____

## I give myself permission to

- ✓ _____
- ✓ _____
- ✓ _____
- ✓ _____
- ✓ _____
- ✓ _____

Pick out the two sentences that have the most impact on you, and write them on the next page. Then hang this somewhere prominent so you see it frequently and are reminded of it frequently.

## Summary

- Find what is keeping you stuck when it comes to money. What's some of the self-talk that holds you back, that takes the wind out of your sails when you try to take on anything to do with money?

- Use the sentence starter "It is safe for me to..." or "I give myself permission to ..." and complete it. Start brainstorming. Write down all options and say them out loud. Notice how you feel when you say them. Continue to tweak the words until you find the right sentence. You'll know it's right when you have a positive physical reaction to it. You might choke up, suddenly take a deep breath, drop your tense shoulders, and feel more relaxed. Pay attention to what happens in your body, and you'll know.

- Once you've found the sentence (or sentences) that resonate, repeat it/them to yourself whenever you can. When you wake up and before you go to bed. When you pay bills. When you deposit money into your account. When you have to have a difficult conversation with someone. When you do something that feels scary. And any time in between.

And don't feel you have to stick with these one or two sentences. As you grow and evolve, that sentence you started with might not have the same effect anymore. If that happens, go back to the drawing board and see if there's another sentence that can help you.

# Chapter 11

# In Closing

We've been on quite a journey to uncover and improve your relationship with money from the inside out. My premise is it's not about the numbers first; it's about how you feel about money, as your feelings shape your perception of what is happening. This is what I refer to as the *human side of money*.

We explored money shame and its impact, delved into the biology of money (including the brain and hormones), and discovered how money stress affects your connection to money. We also examined your money past to understand where your money beliefs originated.

To connect the human side of money to the practical side of money, you gathered all your financial information to get clarity and break free from any financial quicksand you might find yourself in. You also learned how money stress can trigger dopamine-fuelled spending. By identifying the emotions tied to the source of money coming in, you saw how mental accounting can impact your spending habits.

We covered hot potato spending, where you spend money before it even lands in your account—wanting to get rid of it as quickly as possible, like a hot potato.

You found your current financial setpoint in the money thermostat chapter, and you set a new financial setpoint to work towards.

Finally, we looked at the art of spending money from a place of ease, flow and alignment, rather than unconscious patterning. You learned to find the *hell yes* option for what you buy, and that spending is receiving. You saw how conscious receiving goes hand in hand with conscious spending.

Through all the exercises and examples, I hope you now have a better understanding of the human side of money and have gained helpful insights about your own patterns along the way. Once we are free from the triggers and limiting beliefs, and feel worthy of receiving the world, we can stand in a place of power when it comes to money... A place with no shame, uncertainty, guilt and no *shoulds*... a place with trust for the process and trusting that things will work out, while taking full responsibility and being fully accountable. This isn't a perfect place, but a place where missteps are celebrated, as they help us get even more insight into our relationship with money so that we can level up from there!

I know this all may sound like a lot. So, let me put your mind at ease by bringing it back to the main things I hope you receive from reading this book:

**Alignment and clarity are key.**
**Awareness is power.**
**You don't have to be perfect!**
**Money is your friend, here to help you transform your world.**
**Your emotions are essential to it all.**

Because money will be part of your life for the rest of your life, there will always be new insights. And that's a good thing. There will always be new opportunities to adjust your mindset and level up. Every time your life situation, work, income or debt changes, you can reevaluate and adjust.

When you make new decisions, they'll likely also have a financial impact, or they might uncover other emotional triggers to do with money.

With every decision you make, you can now check your *inner* money side first, make sure you're in the right space, and then take action! This way, you can decide confidently and clearly and feel empowered in the process.

Our relationship with money is like an onion with many layers to peel back.

One of my clients, who had done a lot of work on herself already, said after a particularly powerful and life-changing coaching session that by using money as the lens through which to view your life, you cut through all the crap and get straight to the heart of the matter. She said that one session was as helpful as eight years of therapy. Wow!

Working on our relationship with money helps us connect to our core beliefs and fears. Money triggers our primitive brain, where our sense of survival lies.

Our primitive brain is closely linked to the emotional brain, so we kept looking at the emotional side of your relationship with money throughout this book. Since our perception of our financial situation is shaped by how we feel, I hope you always tend to the emotional side FIRST before you make any decisions or take any action.

I wish for you to have had some *aha moments* that are starting to shift in how you relate to money. Even the slightest shift can create a ripple effect that can change your life completely. Celebrate the wins! Embrace the mistakes! It's how we grow, and it's how we get clarity.

I know for a fact that I wouldn't be the person I am today, writing this book for you, had it not been for all the mistakes, setbacks, and challenges in my life. Do the best you can, at any moment.

Returning to the question I asked you in the introduction: "If money were a person, how are you treating it?" Keep working on that answer and build that friendship! Money is your friend, and together, you too can build the life of your dreams.

As I type up the last few pages of this book, I'm sitting in the South of France and have been travelling through Europe for the past year. Together with my dog Scooter, of course!

When I started my journey with money all those years ago, I could have never imagined this could be my life. My financial roller coaster wasn't for the faint of heart. Yet I dug myself out of the trenches, learned and applied what I've shown you in this book, and slowly but surely turned around my situation to where now I am truly living life on my terms. Living my dream life, excited for what's still to come! No more worries about money. No more knots in my stomach. No more restless nights worrying about paying bills.

Someone told me a long time ago that financial freedom is ordering from the left side of the menu, meaning you order whatever you want without looking at the price. That has stuck with me all this time, and to find myself doing exactly that now is so liberating!

This is what I wish for you as well: the freedom to choose what you want, rather than just what you think you can afford.

And, as I've mentioned, it's not about how much money you make or have. There's no magic formula to say that once you make a certain amount of money, you'll be happy and stress-free. Be happy and stress-free at any stage, and the money will follow!

To continue your path, I hope you've joined the Money Wellness Facebook group to connect with like-minded people to share your journey, ask questions and help brainstorm. It's all about the conversations. It will be a safe space to share.

If and when you are ready to take on the practical side of money and learn about an "unbudgeted" way to deal with your money on a day-to-day basis, you can check out The Money Wellness Blueprint course by using the QR code below or the link on the download page.

You will learn how to handle money and set up your finances in a way that fits with the human side of money. The course uses what you've learned about the brain, hormones and beliefs and adds a few key components to set up your behavioural cash flow system and create an easy money flow that feels good, without any effort.

You can use the discount code 'BOOK' to get 35% off as a thank you and celebration that you are taking the next step.

And I would love to hear from you! Let me know how you're doing with money, how the action steps work out for you, or anything else you want to share. You can email me directly at mariska@yourmoneywellness.com.

Looking forward to hearing from you!

## BE WELL. YOU ARE WORTH IT!

## AHA MOMENTS

It's so important to track the insights and aha moments you experience through life, as well as while reading this book. Make sure you keep this sheet handy so you can jot them down right away. Then use this to reflect on it later. You can also use it as a jumping off point for your journalling.

www.ingramcontent.com/pod-product-compliance
Lightning Source LLC
Chambersburg PA
CBHW060558200326
41521CB00007B/609